# The 10 Days

## A Wellness Retreat
### for Personal Transformation
### ...at Home

# Discovering the Recipe for Remarkable Wellness

By

Tonya Kinlow

# The 10 Days

remarkablewellness.us
Published by Royal Perceptions
Edited by Sarajoy Bonebright
ISBN-13: 978-0-9994494-3-1

# Acknowledgments

This book came in phases. Hurried, I self-published as the capstone of a 60 Day Wellness journey I launched with powerful content and energetic power to heal, but shy of the ideal editing. Each time I did *The 10 Days,* I wanted to add more and more.

I want to give my sincere gratitude to Althea Lawton-Thompson, my spiritual coach, who has given me so much needed wisdom and guidance over the last year, including: "You'll never finish the book if you keep wanting to add everything that you are realizing about how God works!" She also walked me through a transcendent experience when I wasn't quite sure if I was losing my mind. To her, I am forever grateful. So today, rewritten, renamed, and republished, I have learned valuable lessons—both spiritual and practical ones—thanks to her guidance.

I also want to thank Althea Jefferson, who encouraged me to expand my vision and jump in whole heartedly. She tells frequently, "I believe in you." That means a lot.

Thank you to my formal and informal editors Sarajoy Bonebright and Deena Daggett, who gave me extra eyes, dealt with my deadlines and again, have shown love at every turn.

Truly, I am blessed.

*For Dayvi.*

# Table of Contents

# Notice

*You are hereby allowed*

*to be happy,*

*to realize your worth,*

*to believe you can do great things,*

*and treat yourself with love and respect.*

**~ Unknown**

# *Introduction*

# THE FUTURE IS CREATED
# IN THE PRESENT.

10 Days… Only 10 days to take your life to the next level and live your highest and best life. Within these pages is the formula to achieving your life's purpose and a profound sense of wellbeing.

This book is the recipe that will animate your personal transformation. For 10 days, you will focus on 7 simple, yet powerful, intentions. These intentions, when combined in the right proportion, are like a recipe that elevates your mindset to a level where you see your purpose with clarity. You will be able to receive divine guidance, and the fears and doubts in your life will begin to disappear. Your path to wellness, happiness, and your full potential will all be made clear.

Take a moment to think about the things in your current life that are getting in the way of the life you want. *The 10 Days* is the time to retreat. The recipe is the method for creating the life of wellness you want. You are provided the ingredients, the measurements, and the amount of time. Here you will utilize your higher senses to reach your higher goals. Your current methods cannot propel you to the happiness you seek.

*The 10 Days* aligns you to your fullest potential day by day, and you will experience remarkable wellness simultaneously. The ingredients are the 7 areas of intention: Meditation, Exercise, Mindful Eating, Self-Care, Rest & Sleep, Journaling & Daily Affirmations, and Kindness & Gratitude. Each ingredient is measured with 24 points. 10 days is the cooking time. Not only will you be transformed, but you will always have the ingredients to live in remarkable wellness.

## Mindset Shift

All real change requires a mindset shift from the old to the new. *Be willing to see things differently.* Alchemy is a magical process of transformation, creation, or combination—a mystical process.

Begin to elevate your thinking to the level of *alchemy*. Spend time with the metaphors to open your mind's eye wider, and elevate your understanding through creativity and instinct…

Imagine a science lab. You are mixing elements and minerals into a glass beaker. You take each ingredient and measure it exactly as indicated in the formula. The proportions are measured just right, some you must agitate, while others must be at a certain temperature.

Then, when each element achieves the perfect molecular structure, you combine them together. The mixture becomes a potion, and its vapor fills the room. As you breathe it in, it clears your vision, like a eucalyptus steam, and now you have pristine clarity and understanding of life, like never before. Everything is illuminated, and you breathe in pure joy and contentment.

However, this feeling is only temporary. It wears off after 24 hours. The only way to hold onto this bliss is to bring your body into natural harmony with these properties. The formula requires persistent focus for 10 days. Then it harmonizes and becomes self-producing within you! And therein lies your personal transformation.

Now imagine you're in the kitchen and are about to bake a cake. You pull out a recipe to guide you. The ingredients have to be measured and then mixed and then placed in the oven to cook. The cooking time will vary based on altitude and the need for all the properties to meld and alchemize into the sweetest version of itself. It transforms. If you take it out too early or too late, you have not achieved your mastery. You wouldn't put a cake in the oven for 10 minutes, then take it out for 10 minutes, and keep putting it back in and out of the oven to let it finish. It would not be edible. It has to cook in the right conditions for the right amount of time. Likewise, *The 10 Days* is the time horizon for your elevation.

This recipe or formula is achieved with the commitment of a Wellness Retreat or vacation. The timeframe is set. The goal is clear. Each day, you are intentional and elevated, and on the 10th day, you are carried above the clouds, and you have built up the spiritual strength to stay in the realm of happiness and wellness. You have built a stamina and the attitudinal muscles to overcome circumstances. You are immune to insanity. However, you have to fly high enough, long enough, to receive these benefits, blessings, and grace.

This book is the magic key that you have been looking for to find the life you of which you have always dreamed How do you *receive* your best guidance? *The 10 Days* is your gift and answer.

Because you are reading these words right now, you have already begun your quest. If you have any belief in a higher power, then trust that this moment of your reading is no mere coincidence. *The 10 Days* came to you in perfect harmony. The method of its delivery and existence is an intentional event in your life. How amazing is it to know you have received the recipe to remarkable wellness?

Knowing *how* a cake is made is different than actually making a cake. Simply reading the ingredients will not bring about transformation. This is not a book you read. This is a book you do. Simply follow the recipe using the 7 areas of daily intentions, and complete it in 10 days.

I am so excited for you to know what I know, and then, you won't be able to help but share it. It is the blessing of giving and receiving. Together, we make the world a better place. It is alchemical.

*"Blessed are the meek, for they shall inherit the earth."*
*– Matthew 5:5*

*Chapter 1*

# ~ MY JOURNEY FROM
# MINDLESS TO MINDFUL ~

I had just returned from a 30th anniversary cruise with my sorority sisters. My Soror Althea implored me to get the message out to the world about mindful living, wellness, and inspiration right away! She pushed and pushed, and my excitement grew. My wheels quickly turned. We made plans to combine my newly minted, yet practical, Certified Health Coach Certification with the higher inspiration of spirituality and mindfulness that I had already been speaking on for years.

Then Sonia, who was also on the cruise, told me that she had received a "word" for me: that God had amazing plans for me and that He wanted me to go outside my comfort zone so He could take me to my next level of excellence. She said that I had been playing it too safe for too long.

Time is a funny concept, because in about a millisecond, I excavated through my life events of the last 3 years, to see if there was any truth in what she had said.

Let's see... I had quit a cushy lucrative corporate executive career to create a business that would promote healthy living to the world via an app. That was crazy risky! I endured rejection from investors that did not have faith in me. *That* showed vulnerability and courage. And as a lifelong financial professional, I am betting my retirement on a moonshot idea. This is monumental risk taking for me. So, no. I'm not playing it safe.

I knew I had to take my thinking to a higher level based on who the question came from, and who the question came through. So in the next millisecond, I opened up my emotional guidance system, and with one deep breath, all of my heart energy and my intuition were on deck. *Tonya, where are you playing it safe? Where do you desire more degrees of freedom?* I reminded myself that there are only two emotions: fear and love. You can always simplify whatever is vexing you, by determining which lens you are using.

My true self zoomed in like a rocket and inhabited my body with awareness. I straightened and realized that I fear people thinking I'm too "out there" or that I might be going too far on my spiritual journey. Meditation, intuitive guidance, walking in faith? People may think I've gotten soft and lost my mind. They want to know, "Who does she think she is, and what gives her the qualifications to think she can offer any guidance on living your best life of pursuing your highest calling?" Basic imposter syndrome stuff.

Sonia said, "My sister, *you* are overqualified. You have to share your story so that fear can disappear." Wow. I got chills. God did send a word for me after all.

So, I worked through my fears and began to tell my story publicly. This is why I am qualified. It took me 12 years to arrive at this place of peace and purpose from a place of *total chaos*! I want everyone to know it is possible to have contentment in your life and, better yet, how to get there.

Here is my story…

I hid the embarrassment of an abusive marriage, battled through a bitter divorce, and suffered quietly through depression and alcoholism. Separated from my kids, I endured incredible mother's guilt and judgment from my own family, society at large, and, to be honest, even from myself. In the midst of it all, my kids were in a tragic car accident, where my son almost died and is, to this day, paralyzed. I spent months in hospitals. My best friend, Toi, took me in, when I had no job, a dwindling bank account, and a future that looked really, really bleak.

I didn't know it then, but I know it know. It was my faithfulness to these key ingredients in *The 10 Days* that kept me pressing through each day, trying to get to the other side—to happiness. I didn't know that I was creating my own blocks by not forgiving. *How do you practice forgiveness and gratitude when everything has turned upside down? Thankful for what? Forgive who?* You see, I didn't have role models for this messy stuff. My parents are still married; domestic violence is a dirty little secret; and I never knew anyone with a disability.

Fast forward…

It wasn't easy, and it took over a decade, one day at a time. I landed, though. I got a better job at a great company, making phenomenal money. I married a man who treats me like the queen that I am. My son has inspired thousands with his charming personality and thirst for life, while traversing a severe disability. Both of my kids have moved into their own homes and are living independently. (Hallelujah!) I'm healthy, beautiful, and, yes, now wise.

I'm incredibly excited to share *The 10 Days* to remarkable wellness so you can let go of fear. This is both a retreat and a recipe that produces a mindset shift that takes you above your fears, shows you they are not real, and gives you the confidence to take the disruptive steps needed to get to complete wellness. Don't worry about it all right away. Just read this book. Take in each page, one at a time, and you will chart your path to your best life without fear and without breaking the bank.

### Finding Purpose

I've attended countless retreats. I had collected decades of pain, stress, and fear, and thousands of dollars in travel to follow some of the best spiritual leaders on the planet. I've been on a quest for freedom from the stress of the world, for happiness, and for my purpose.

If you're searching, I'm going to tell you your purpose now. Search no more. It is the same as mine and everyone else's on the planet. *Your purpose is to radiate and realize your full potential, with your talents connected and in harmony with all that God has for you.* Your only job then, is to align your talents with the Universe, and there is where you will experience complete wellbeing. That is what you will be doing in *The 10 Days*. The recipe will put you in alignment. Your fears will fall away like dust.

It was after my friends nudged me that I faced my own fears and began to really take risks. These were perceived risks, which is what fear is. I prayed, *Shower down on me, Lord, shower down.* I did *The 10 Days*, and I live in excitement for the next moment, without fear. I am free. And so He did as promised, and my cup runneth over. He is blessing the reader of these words right now, as well. The recipe is your journey above fear, and it has already begun.

*"For I know the plans I have for you," declares*
*the LORD, "plans to prosper you and not to harm*
*you, plans to give you hope and a future."*
*– Jeremiah 29:11*

# Notes & Epiphanies

# Chapter 2

## ~ THE AT-HOME
## WELLNESS RETREAT ~

The goal of *The 10 Days* is not to lose weight, although you will. The goal is not to become an enlightened master, although your inner spirit will shine more brightly. The goal of this retreat is to excavate through the habits and negative thoughts that keep you bound to your grief, fears, and insecurities, and then to lift your decision-making to align with your highest potential and greatest wellbeing.

This book is a guided retreat to remarkable wellness that you will customize, based on your own lifestyle. You will receive the recipe that contains a structure of activities to keep your mind empty of the clutter of the outside world so that you can instead focus on your best life. You determine your level of commitment to transforming your life into one of peace and joy. Then, using this guide for 10 days, you will make your wellness journey a priority, giving attention to your eating, self-care, lifestyle, stillness, and health.

Over the last several years, I have attended many wellness retreats in exotic places—all to relax and unwind, to "find" myself, to recuperate and forget about work and feelings of stress, and to be immersed in culture, nature, history, or whatever distraction that could bring me peace at the time. I also found it almost impossible to (re)integrate all of the peace and bliss of vacation back into everyday life for more than a few weeks. I needed something that would stick, and I wondered, *how can we hold onto that feeling of wellbeing every day?*

The good news is that when you find that inner peace leaving you, you can transform where you are. You don't need to go away on vacation to find yourself.

This book is your personal Wellness Retreat, devoted to higher consciousness practices, equipping you to rise above your problems and to begin to manifest extraordinary results—all in the comfort of your own home. Transformation does not need to be expensive. Transformation is a journey within, without distance, and closer than your next breath.

It's time to check into your own spa for 10 days to unveil an astonishing transformation. Let your friends and family know that you are going on your wellness journey retreat, just like any other vacation. With a little planning, retreat to a place where you are the center of the Universe. Close your eyes. There you are.

*"What you seek is seeking you."*

*– Rumi*

# Notes & Epiphanies

*Chapter 3*

# ~ MINDSET SHIFT TO WILLINGNESS ~

What would you do if you could not remember the past? How would you feel if you couldn't see yourself in the mirror and your looks didn't matter? What dreams would you choose to pursue if you weren't held back by self-limiting thoughts? Who would you be? Who are you? Get ready to transform into the real you. You can do and be anything you want. You have to create the type of perspective that supports your choices.

This is for anyone who has looked in the mirror and thought, *I don't recognize myself anymore.* It's time to recalibrate and get back to the you that you used to know—the you who has easy friendships, instead of toxic relationships—the you who spent more time in love and laughter, than mistrust and mayhem.

The fact that you picked up this book is confirmation that it is time for you to get away from it all and transform back into the real you. There are no coincidences; there are no accidents.

## *Mindset Shift Visualization*

Take yourself back to that time in your childhood when you had no worries. Go as far back as you need to. Were you five? Maybe you were two. Maybe it was your birthday. Feel who you were *before* you experienced injustice, betrayal, money woes, death, or disease. Remember how it felt when everything was just everything—not good or bad, but just how things were. Feel your heart lighten as you go back to a time before judgment and before the world convinced you that you weren't enough and that if you weren't worried then you weren't prepared. Let's agree that was a time of innocence. Every one of us has that in common, even if it was only the first day we were born.

I tell you this: That innocence is still within you. Layers and layers of barriers have been erected around it to protect you from the evils of the world. Unfortunately, while built on good intentions to protect you, they also have wreaked havoc by keeping you from that feeling of peace and innocence.

Now you've reached a point that you crave peace and you're starving to find it, but you don't know how. You can transcend these walls altogether to get back to your innocence. That is where your peace is.

I remember most vividly the innocence of my childhood from the times when I was sick. I knew, beyond a shadow of a doubt, that my mother was going to make me better. I had only to tell her where it hurt. For the common cold, it was going to be orange juice, vitamin C, soup, and lots of love. For a tummy ache, maybe ginger ale and crackers. For scrapes and burns and poison ivy rashes to mosquito bites, she had just the right salves. For concussions, sprains, or any other malady, she had some type of wisdom that, if you only followed her directions, everything would get better.

Mom would set up a special room in the house, where I would be comfortable and not be bothered by the activity of 4 siblings, their neighborhood friends, and busy parents. She created a sanctuary to sleep and rest and recover. Through the beautiful combination of isolation and attention that I now recognize as stillness, my mother gave me one of the secrets to healing. This is the formula that I give to you for your transformation. Visualize the health and restoration that comes from rest.

Rest without worry. This simple sentence contains two critical mindset shifts. First, it is imperative to prioritize rest as a crucial intention in your life. You actually come back stronger each day after a period of rest and restoration.

Sleep deprivation is a silent killer and literally a mood depressant. Second, don't worry. *A Course in Miracles*, Lesson 48 says, "There is nothing to fear. The presence of fear is a sure sign that you are trusting in your own strength" (instead of God's). This all by itself would be transformational… learning to rest without worry. And there is so much more grace to receive.

I hope this shift sounds like music to your ears.

*"It's simple, but it's not easy."*
*– Evan Campbell*

## Meet the Inner Victim

It's time to look in the mirror and greet yourself. Literally, take 5 minutes and go gaze into your own eyes for 5 minutes, repeating the question, "Who am I?"

Allow your mind and spirit to open up to the infinite possibilities of what you have yet to accomplish. Embrace the fact that there is so much more good coming your way, and all you have to do is identify your self-limiting beliefs and choose your thoughts differently. You will know how to do this in *The 10 Days*.

Unwind and shed the stress that's coming at you. Stop worrying about money, who's mistreating you, your boss, job insecurity, your kids, your parents, and all of it. Worry will not add one day to your life.

## Answer these questions:

➤ Have you been treated unfairly or cruelly?

➤ Are your life circumstances causing you to implode?

➤ Do you feel incomplete, insecure, or like an imposter?

➤ Are you waiting for a future event to make you happy?

➢ Have you been damaging your health and relationships by overworking?

➢ Are you constantly stressed?

➢ Do you compulsively blame or procrastinate?

If you answered yes to any of these questions, meet your inner victim. Just know that this negativity is the conditioning of the world which keeps us separated from our own greatness. In this retreat, we choose differently. We consciously choose to shift our mindset to one of positivity and light, and away from the dark and the pessimistic side of what is possible.

Essentially, you have been choosing to stay in the comfort zone of "sameness" even though it makes you unhappy. You have been afraid to confront the changes you need, because they will disrupt your lifestyle. Begin to understand right now that you have to disrupt your current habits to create the actual lifestyle and wellness that you desire. Why are you afraid to put yourself first and eat right and exercise when you know it will help you lose the weight you want? Why do you think your job or family won't support micro shifts in your schedule to improve your own well-being? Have you even asked? Ask.

Shift your mindset. Trust me, if you tell the people in your life that you were immersing yourself in improving your overall health for the next 10 days, the honorable and true will support you. In this day in age, they would probably reward you, and be inspired by your transformation.

## *Is fear irrational?*

You want the mindset to confront your fear. Any resistance that you have to achieving your total wellbeing is, at its core, based on fear, and that's all it is. Fear is blocking your clear path to happiness. You have the power to rise above the level of your circumstances. In fact, you have infinitely more potential to overcome anything life presents to you—anything.

The tools to overcome deep levels of insecurities on a spiritual level are all the same. There are only 2 emotions with which to make your decisions: fear and love. In this retreat, you will learn how to overcome fear, and make the shift to your highest and best decisions out of love.

A past CEO gives this advice on giving presentations: "If you're not worried, then you're probably under-prepared." I received that advice, and I really took it to heart. Now, I know it's a load of garbage. That simple influence from someone I respected kept me stressed for decades. This is how the conditioning of the world misguides us from our inner peace. I *thought* it was a good thing.

When you are present, pulling from your inner guidance and being your best self, you don't need to worry. You can speak authentically. This is why people who speak without notes and who tell you their stories are so relatable. They don't have to tear through layers of ego, theirs or yours, to make a real connection with you. The energy of the connection reaches you like the steam and aroma rising from a cup of healing tea. You can't avoid it; it is received effortlessly.

Everything you need is already within you. You will draw on these higher practices whenever you feel yourself slipping into old habits that don't serve your best interests. This works whether you are re-integrating from a retreat or if you simply need to meet yourself where you are. This is the journey without distance. This is your transformation.

## *Why should I transform?*

Life conditions us to believe in certain things that do not align with what we really want. This misalignment causes stress and unhappiness. Therefore, the goal of transformation is to release all of the conditioning that has been built up as a barrier to keep you from being your true self. You are the conscious creator of your life. If you want to change your life situation, you start by addressing how you think about your life.

Ask yourself, *What does success mean to me?* Has your definition brought you happiness, and where are you stuck? Usually, these barriers cannot be seen with the naked eye, yet they are as real as a brick wall.

The goal is to transcend and overcome these layers, brick by brick, and transform back into your authentic self. It's worth saying again:

You. Are. Enough. Already. You have everything within you to be happy, healthy, and at peace with yourself. It's time to knock down the wall.

These barriers look different in everyone. They are the destructive things we do outwardly to avoid the feeling of emptiness. Excessive drinking, overeating, shopping, gambling, partying, and drugs are a few popular examples. These barriers leave us drained emotionally and physically, and they cast us into a deeper pit of guilt, depression, regret, and isolation. Left unchecked, our bodies suffer inflammation and then result in physical problems like migraines, illnesses, and disease.

The word "retreat" is defined as "movement away from a place or situation, especially because it is dangerous or unpleasant." That is exactly right for our purposes. To get to where we are going, we have to leave where we have been. First, we must retreat, then we move forward, and then we transform.

During *The 10 Days*, you will have the opportunity to put your phone away, immerse yourself in self-care, get out of your regular rut or routine, dedicate yourself to personal growth, and learn insightful techniques to bolster your personal practice.

**The benefits you experience will include:**

- Inner peace

- Higher energy

- Long-term healing

- Serenity

- Improved mobility

Take time to really think about how your life circumstances are causing upset in your life. Transformation for lasting change is a holistic approach. It is 360 degrees of commitment. You will face any feelings of fear (separation, guilt, negativity, and more) that are creating defensiveness and illness.

To truly transform, we address all of these factors squarely, which can be tiresome, but oh so rewarding. Our ultimate goal is to banish what I call False Evidence Appearing Real: F.E.A.R.

We have fallen into a culture of shaming our bodies. But with inspiration from your most important values, you can achieve and maintain that vibrancy you really desire, and then the weight on the scale won't matter.

---

*"When you change the way you see things,*
*the things you see change."*
*– Wayne Dyer*

---

Take the time to jot down any additional desires here to hold your intentions as you journey forward. Use this book as your personal tour guide. This is not a book for sharing. It is your personal guidance system and confidant. Consider it your trusted friend and companion, where you can confide your innermost treasured insights. I encourage you to highlight, scribble in the margins liberally, and use the pages at the end of each chapter to capture insights. These are epiphanies to return to as signposts along your journey.

We are essentially all battling the same problems. We are, in essence, all the same. Look at the following list and check the areas where you are seeking solutions, and jot down additional ones.

- Stress Relief
- Spiritual Nourishment
- Relaxation
- Weight Loss
- Physical Healing
- Beating Depression
- Strengthen Relationships
- _____
- _____

*A Course in Miracles* says that we think we have problems, but we only really have one: our separation from God. I understand this to mean that ultimately when we fill our thinking and choices with love, peace, and wisdom in stillness, we rid ourselves of all perceived problems. Ultimately, that's it. What would God do?

## *Questioning Deeply*

A major problem-solving tool is called the Root Cause Analysis. Simply ask the question "Why?" 5 times in exploration to get to the root cause of the problem. I find it is a helpful tool in all situations. Try this technique to really get to the heart of what blocks you, and it will direct you to the beginning of your journey's path. Your neural pathways will begin to change to deeper way of understanding life— not just surface stuff. Your mindset will have more depth and richness to tease out and receive important guidance.

If you're extremely stressed at work, it's not just because you hate your job. That's the simple answer to the first "Why?". If your boss is an unreasonable dictator, well, that's the reason to the second "Why?".

Transformation requires internal awareness. You are not going to transform your boss. The problem is the distance you hold *yourself* apart from happiness.

For the third "Why?" you may be tempted to huff, "Well, I don't know why my boss is an ass!" Our inner victim can be formidable.

A good third question would be, "Why do I let my boss get to me?"

Now we're getting somewhere. Going within the "I" is the answer. You begin to discontinue the constant projection on external factors. Perhaps he makes you feel vulnerable.

The fourth and fifth "Why?" questions will really get you to some meaningful answers. Self-exploration is the first step toward your own awareness.

Another benefit of transformation is you will live your best life without continually singing the "how somebody did me wrong" song. When you transform, you become the master of your fate, and never again will you blame anyone for your life's circumstances.

Your focus will turn away from other people's pettiness to higher thinking. You will begin to address your own inner demons and live in the discovery of life's vital questions about purpose, existence, and themes of compassion and unconditional love. Inner reflection and stillness will excavate through the barriers of lifelong conditioning.

At the beginning of your retreat, start with your "Why?" (goal) squarely in mind. Your awareness is everything. With it, and an open mindset, you will get to the root cause. The barriers will fall away, and your spirit will be restored. Ask and you will receive. It is time to surrender, transcend, and transform.

*"This is the confidence we have in approaching*
*God: that if we ask anything according to his will,*
*he hears us."*
*– 1 John 5:14*

# Notes & Epiphanies

# Chapter 4:

## ~ BEGINNING YOUR
## WELLNESS RETREAT ~

Transformation is not reserved for people who have lots of money and time to take these wellness excursions and vacations. I saved my pennies and used all my (and friends') frequent flyer miles to get to these retreats, because I was on a desperate search for inner peace. While I did have major awakenings, I found that reintegration into home life was challenging. Maintaining that spaciousness in my soul and practicing the universal principles was difficult to hold onto for more than a couple of months—sometimes even a couple of days!

At some point, I would find myself back in self-doubt and familiar frustrations. While the impact and experience of these spiritual retreats cannot be denied as one of my life's greatest, I simply cannot afford to constantly go on retreats to build up my spirit man.

The wellness industry is approaching $1 trillion and is growing twice as fast as the global economy. However, you do not need to go broke following a spiritual leader at a 5-star resort to meditate, zip-line, or walk on hot coals to "awaken." The key, then, is to replicate that experience and commune with higher consciousness all the time in every day busy life. I can't just go quit my job, leave my family, and move to a beautiful island, meditating and contemplating all day.

## How do I maintain peace?

Well, this is the question, isn't it? You have to develop the discipline to maintain balance, even when the world around you is erratic. This takes practice.

In *The 10 Days* you will not just learn the steps to transform, you will *do* them. You cannot understand the principles to achieving the life you want by only reading about them. Experience is necessary to infuse these principles to your psyche. Then you will not only have peace, but you will radiate your joy from within to be an inspiration to others.

I attended a Shamanic retreat in Sedona and had experiences that were other-worldly. I could feel the vibration of energy vortexes that affect nature and my perception of time and space. There I met a wonderful healer from South Africa, named Lucky, who gave me the advice I try to live with daily. I email her sometimes just to make sure she is real. She said in her beautifully thick accent, "Tonya, just stay warm. Don't get too hot, nor too cold. Just always stay warm." That struck me right between the eyes, Lucky.

What she was telling me was that wild swings from happiness to depression, and from terrific anger to peace, are not the way. Yet this is how I was taught to live my life. Who knew? Working long hours, competing relentlessly for the next promotion, and experiencing a constant guilt of the absent working mother was the norm. Insanity!

Nothing was ever quite right. I was always swinging from high-highs to low-lows, and I thought this was what it took to have a successful life. Likewise, I thought my first marriage was normal because of the laughter, partying, and traveling. Hot! Until the celebrations were followed with fights and abuse of the same intensity. Cold.

Warm is the place. Warm and cozy, love and light, that is where you maintain peace. In the flow of love, never straying too far off the course that God has for you, the zone is warm. You can find your zone and your flow in your own retreat...*at home!*

## *What must I give up?*

You have to be willing to see things differently. You have to give up the notion that you are wrong or that you are above or beneath anyone else. Give up attachments.

The world says there is a right way to do things and a wrong way. In the spirit, there is no duality; all things are possible. Be open to being amazed and awed. Live in wonderment, like a child, with a brand-new beginner's mind. You only have to give up your attachment to the past.

It is important when you want to make changes that last a lifetime that you learn things in your own way. Here, the common themes that permeate religion, higher consciousness, and tools of our time will return you back into your best self.

*The framework for your success is here, but it will only work if you give yourself permission to be the number one priority in your life and do The 10 Days. This is the most important premise of this book for actual personal growth and inner transformation.*

You must agree that you want to transform into your best self and get unstuck. You must also be willing to drop the baggage, get rid of your bad habits, and get closer to your higher power.

Basically, you agree that you want what we all want: to have peace and happiness. If you agree, go ahead and commit, and sign your name right here.

*I am deeply committed to improving my life. I will retreat from my daily perceived barriers to do The 10 Days and ultimately experience personal transformation and remarkable wellness.*

*Signature:* _____          *Date:*_____

Buddhism says that suffering is normal, and that it can be overcome by understanding the *4 Noble Truths* and following the *8-Fold Path*. Other religions believe that suffering and guilt are signs of dedication to holiness and rebuking of sin, and then you atone. There are many constructs for how to live harmoniously, but your goal is to see clearly what the world has given you.

Go deep within to find what the Universe or God wants for you. Begin to live your life, recognizing where there are gaps and striving for alignment. That is your transformation. That is huge. That is the goal of spiritual leaders and religions since the beginning of time: to guide humankind back to its source, which is God.

## *What will I gain?*

You will find reconciliation and alignment. Consider this transformation as your tour guide, but your travel, the pictures you take, and your accommodations are all yours. This is intimately your experience. Only you can choose what transportation is best for your peace and happiness.

In a Universe of infinite possibilities, of course there are infinite prisms with which to view life. Words are inadequate and tend to vaporize. True understanding transcends this realm and is more about living in the fragrance of what the words tried to convey after the perfume dissipates. We all have to evolve.

There are times when understanding happens immediately, like a flash of lightning. However, transformation and illumination of your true spirit is a journey that never ends. Only your peace increases every day for the rest of your life.

Sounds good, right? Well, let's get into the heart of the retreat. There are central truths that run through all religions, such as love, higher power, the oneness of all things, and compassion for one's neighbors. These are the same themes that cultivate wellness. They embody the pure definition of wellbeing.

Every holistic wellness program will have some, if not all, of these practices so that you can also embody the truth of your own life—your purpose. These intentions are proven throughout time and space. You now have the formula to remarkable wellness that you can achieve at home and for the rest of your life.

There are 7 Areas of Intentions that you will commit to during this 10-day reset. Think of the intentions as a collage that mystically fits together.

The components are:

1. Meditation

2. Exercise

3. Mindful Eating

4. Self-Care

5. Journaling & Daily Affirmations

6. Kindness & Gratitude

7. Rest & Sleep

The best place to transform is right where you are. All of the greatest works on higher consciousness speak to *presence* as the path to your highest self and to your higher power. You will gain control of your life through surrender.

Only you can choose to eat the foods that keep your head clear and your temperament even. Only you can move enough to keep your body vibrant and healthy. Only you can meditate so that you can slow your thoughts down enough to hear what God has for you.

You don't need to travel. Your transformation is closer than your next breath. You can do it right where you are. It will set the stage for an open life where you can receive constant guidance on being your best self, wherever you are.

---

*"Be still and know that I am God."*
*– Psalm 46:10*

---

## What does success look like?

The measure of success is your transformation. It's being able to trust a process that promises to cleanse your body and open your soul so that you can become the person that you want to be—the person you are searching for. Let the real you that is already held within your heart and spirit be the leader of your life decisions.

You will break the barriers and reconnect with your innocence. The reality is that the innocent spirit within you is much more resilient than the world gives it credit for, and it should be given the lead in your life. You have to trust it.

You will no longer use brute force, accompanied with worry and stress, to muscle through life. You will now come into yourself and find the peace where a happy life happens. Life will flow. It doesn't look like your bank account or your pants size. It's the life you are meant to experience.

You have everything you need. You will transform into your real self. There are 3 Understandings your new mindset must grasp to make this retreat powerful. In the next chapter you will learn how these 3 critical universal laws work. Then you will use these laws during the 10 days of your retreat to your benefit, which is why they exist. Your life will begin to flow.

---

*"Let nothing frighten you.*
*All things pass away.*
*God never changes.*
*Patience obtains all things.*
*He who has God, finds he lacks for nothing.*
*God alone suffices."*
*– Teresa of Avila*

---

# Notes & Epiphanies

# Chapter 5

## ~ THE 3 UNDERSTANDINGS ~

There are 3 foundational themes to embrace to really participate in your own unfoldment. More times than I can count I have "boxed with God." I prayed for what I wanted and didn't understand when I didn't get it, or I ended up shaking my fist at the sky because something horrible happened. Whatever happened to "Ask and you shall receive?"

For years, I have been reading, studying, praying, meditating, and doing many of the things you will find in this book to get to an answer to how this works. How can I find happiness, have my prayers answered, and find my true purpose and wellbeing?

As clearly as possible, I'm going to give you what I call "The 3 Understandings," to show you metaphorically how the Universe works and your significant importance within this framework.

Please note: Understanding is not *knowing*. You can understand something, like what forgiveness means, without knowing forgiveness, because you are holding grudges against those who hurt your feelings. Understanding is an intellectual connection to information being received. It's "aha!" moments.

The 3 Understandings lay the foundation for you to reach your higher consciousness. From there, it is up to you to do the work of infusing these understandings into your everyday life and living the life you desire. Then you can *know* and be the wisdom and peace you crave.

## *Understanding #1*

You have to have a basic understanding of the laws of the Universe. *Understanding #1 is the Universe is an interwoven network we are all one and interconnected.*

Imagine a fabric where all the thread is interconnected and creates an heirloom of intricate design. That is the Universe, and you are a thread within it. Each thread is important. Your prayers and actions mix in with the prayers and actions of others, and they become one universal action, made up of an infinite amount of mini-actions and intentions.

This is why it is powerful when more than 2 people come together for an intercession. You are not alone, no matter how alone you may feel. We are all one. In the spirit (or quantum), there is no place where you (and your choices) end, and I begin. My choices and actions have resonance with the other ~8 billion people on the planet at any given moment, and any given situation is the result of all of those interactions.

Imagine a big pot of soup. You think of yourself as an important ingredient to the soup and try to stand alone. But you have to change your thinking to see that your role is the most integral when you work within the soup to enhance the flavors and make it the most delicious, delectable thing that's ever been tasted.

Your role is critical, not by standing alone, but by bringing together the creation of flavors, tastes, textures, and forms. Alone, you're just an onion. Without you, the soup can't be its best self, lacking flavor. In this understanding of the Universe, you and I are the soup.

The Universe is like the air we breathe. It connects us all.

## *Understanding #2*

This is a popular scripture that is frequently used:

---

*"For everyone who asks, receives; the one who seeks finds; and the one who knocks, the door will be opened."*
*— Matthew 7:8*

---

But, for the life of me, if this is true, then why, why, *why* don't I have everything I've ever wanted?! Why do war and hunger exist, and why don't I have that nice house, fancy car, and big bank account?

Two reasons:

1. Prayers enter into the quantum and do not exist in a vacuum (back to Understanding #1), and

2. Taken alone, that scripture is out of context.

The following scripture is a little more encompassing:

*"I am the vine. You are the branches. If you
remain in me and I in you, you will bear much
fruit; apart from me you can do nothing. If you do
not remain in me, you are like a branch that is
thrown away and withers; such branches are
thrown into the fire and burned. If you remain in
me and my words remain in you, ask whatever you
wish, and it will be done for you."*
*– John 15:5-7*

*Understanding #2 is if you remain (abide) in God's Word, the Universal Law, then you can ask and receive.* If you don't, you might only wither away. This is also called The Law of Attraction, or Karma, Cause and Effect, The Golden Rule… however you receive it.

Words often aren't sufficient, but the question here is this: Are you living a life that God has called you to? If you don't know what that is, don't worry. It will start to be revealed to you during this retreat. Your job is simply to abide.

When you are not receiving what you are asking for, spend time contemplating where you need to abide so that what you request can be done for you. What does it mean to abide? The word "abide" means to "uphold, keep, comply, remain, stay, act in accord with, submit to, remain steadfast or faithful to."

## *Understanding #3*

*Understanding #3 is that when you set your desires and intentions into the tapestry of the Universe through prayer and meditation, you can release it, and it will manifest.* You don't even need to worry about it anymore—simply go about your day-to-day practical steps of action.

Our tapestry is in a constant state of design and redesign, and your intention will be woven into the fabric of all that *is*. Maybe you're the extra texture—an embroidered rose, a delicate leaf, lace around the edges, etc. The only way to truly transform is to consciously change the design of your essential being. Participate in your own unfolding. In doing so, you improve the entire blanket. Don't just be carried along by the blanket. Participate in its design.

Jump ahead to Chapter 14 and read "Thinking Stuff" for a more poetic interpretation from *The Science of Getting Rich* by Wallace Wattles.

When we understand that we are all one and interconnected by our choices, then we are able to abide within the divine laws (love, forgiveness, gratitude, kindness, *and* Karma). Every day and all day, be aware of your connections with all things, abide in love and compassion always, and set your intentions through prayer and presence. Then the Universe will not only answer your prayers, but will exceed all of your wildest imaginings.

With these 3 Understandings, you will come to realize that when you bless others, you are also being kind to yourself; and when you are kind to yourself, you are a blessing to the world. This is how you improve your wellness, relationships, home, and job and achieve all the things your heart desires. This is also how you bless others and make the world a better place. It is a win-win scenario.

Spend quiet time cleaning your body and clearing your mind, to let these 3 Understandings take hold in your spirit, and set you on the pathway to your higher self, happiness, and wellbeing.

# Notes & Epiphanies

## Chapter 6

## ~ THE PLANNING PRACTICALITIES ~

Your home transformation journey is 24 hours a day for 10 days. Sleep is a very important part. The scheduling and planning will start prior to the retreat. Schedule some time off work if possible, like you would on any retreat or vacation. This 10 days is a big deal in the evolution of your life. Give it homage. Find babysitters, go grocery shopping, and make appointments to pamper yourself. Self-care is also extremely important on this retreat.

Consider this pre-planning an integral part of the journey. In no way do you want to be overwhelmed during the 10 days by planning. Everything that happens is meant to happen, and you can go with the flow better with fewer curve balls.

Find a time when you're not traveling and can commit to 8 hours of sleep or total silence every day. This is an extraordinary process. You want to incorporate as much presence into your daily life, which includes rest and quiet so that you can retreat away from the daily grind.

This transformation is like on-the-job training, where you're learning and applying what you've learned throughout the day. You only need to have faith the size of a mustard seed of faith to ask the Universe for exactly what you are desiring.

---

*"All hard work brings a profit, but mere talk leads*

*only to poverty."*

*— Proverbs 14:23*

---

This transformation will last the rest of your lifetime, but let's focus on the first 10 days, shall we?

## Transformation Preparation To-Do List

Literally, use this as your checklist and check the boxes to ensure you are ready for an amazing experience.

☐ **Budget**

How much would you spend to achieve peace and happiness? That's what these five-star retreats ask you. I'm here to tell you it doesn't have to cost anything. It could be as low as $100 for books or organic groceries or as high as thousands of dollars if you choose daily luxury 90-minute massages. This is up to you. I chose the middle of the road. I did my at home retreat for under $500. Waaayyy cheaper than my wellness retreats in Costa Rica!

☐ **Self-Care**

I treated myself to a mani one day, and then a pedi the next day to break up the experiences ($75). I hadn't had a facial in years ($50). I took bubble baths with all the fixin's, like candles, aromatherapy, bubbles, and a book. (YASSS, free!). I burned 3 candles practically all the time that I was at home ($20). I made body creme from essential oils mixed with cocoa butter and shea butter—so wonderful ($40)! I went to a pottery studio and made ceramic bowls ($60). I used an inexpensive local spa that charged $50 for a 60-minute massage. Over the 10 days, I had 2 massages and 1 facial and several bubble baths. The intentional quality and quantity of self-love is sheer delight all by itself!

☐ **Media (Books, Journals & Videos)**

Unread self-help books line my shelves, so no additional money there. I'm sure you have a few lying around too. A journal is $10. I think you get the picture.

☐ **Schedule Appointments**

- *Doctor Appointments*

Schedule in advance for the 10-Day Transformation. Even if the appointments are not available during the transformation period, you make energetic progress toward your wellbeing. These could be your annual physical, dentist appointment, OB/GYN, prostate, dermatology, or anything. Go ahead and schedule and prioritize appointments that you have been putting off and things you have been wanting to look into.

- *Spa Treatments*

Pamper yourself with as many as you can afford during this period. Spread them out over the course of the 10 days. In a typical spa weekend you may get a massage, a mani, a pedi, a facial and or a wrap. Try not to bundle, but rather to experience something new every day. Get a massage one day. Then your nails the next day. Maybe another massage and then the pedicure the day after that. Shake things up, yet give focus to each pleasant experience singularly.

## ☐ **Collect Media**

- *Select Reading Materials*

Purchase the books you want to read on this journey. A recommended reading list is provided in the back of this book to get you started. As with all decisions, go within and ask for guidance, and the perfect items to help you for your journey will practically jump out at you.

- *Select Visual Content*

Try to watch comedies and light-hearted movies. This is for play—to keep your spirits up and elevated. This is to counteract the seriousness and burden that has grown and weighed you down without even noticing it. Stay far away from violent content. If you identify with any of these things below, you are predisposing yourself to drama, anxiety, and stress without even realizing it. Stop it.

- News junkie

- Horror movie fan

- Action flicks with violence buff

- Songs with explicit content

*Determine a news source.*

Keep news updates to a minimum, or avoid it altogether. The news overwhelmingly focuses on the negative. Turn off notifications and commit to checking current events once per day, if at all. Trust me, if anything major happens, your family and friends will let you know.

## ☐ **Purchase a Journal**

Writing is its own therapy. It is the conversation with you and You (with a big Y). Ideally, you will write, not type, your daily musings with the ancient method of ink to paper. It's the feel of paper, the color of the ink, the smell of the room that will also come alive when you write your thoughts. Doodle in the margins. Color. Create whatever you wish, but do it at least once daily, and as often as you wish, capture your thoughts and feelings. Creativity is the medium through which we express our life's purpose. If you don't believe you are creative, you are stunting your own growth.

I used to say this all the time: I'm not creative. I was a finance person. Numbers were my language. I didn't give myself credit for designing and sewing my own clothes, curating wonderful art in my home, or creating positive solutions and outcomes on my job.

The truth is that everyone is creative. Journaling will pull out your intimate thoughts and let your individual creativity surface. Focus on levity, laughter and love. Choose your movies, music, and books based on their energetic ability to actively support the rise of uplifting your spirit.

## ☐ **<u>Determine Food Choices</u>**

Commit how you will eat. I recommend whole foods and an all-natural diet. Lean heavily toward organic to avoid the toxins from pesticides. Basically, keep it simple. Smoothies for snacks or meal replacements is a great addition to a traditional diet.

Make your food commitment, and write it at the bottom of this page so that you don't forget or sway during the 10-day period. Eating clean is essential to your overall health and wellbeing. I encourage you NOT to count carbs, calories, or fat. Your focus should be on your spirit and overall wellbeing. This is not a diet.

With that said, here is a simple plan that almost everyone can adhere to that will be holistically beneficial. Please check with your doctor before beginning any new eating regimens. You can eat anything you want EXCEPT for these 4 things:

1. **White Flour**

2. **Alcohol**

3. **Sugar**

4. **Processed Foods**

Use the W.A.S.P. pneumonic to remember. That is, No W.A.S.P.

Everything in moderation is good for you. Natural, organic vegetables and fruits can be eaten in abundance. Yes, fruit has natural sugar and carbs, and yes, this is why it is the nectar of the gods!

This is a healthy way of living that you can incorporate into daily life as you go forward. Many detoxes say no coffee, no meat, no dairy, etc. You decide those things. If you want a little cream in your coffee, you know your formula. Your knowledge of your body and the foods you like and dislike will lead you to your ultimate eating plan.

There are plenty of people out there trying to tell you what to eat, and quite frankly, it's basically easier to know what *not* to eat. Set your clean-eating intention, clear out the cabinets, and go get some good groceries.

*Write it down here.*

*I am committed to eliminating these foods during the 10 days:*

1. _____

2. _____

3. _____

## ☐ Reduce Technology Time

Americans check their phone on average once every 12 minutes—burying their heads in their phones 80 times a day, according to new research. A study by the global tech protection and support company, Asurion, found that the average person struggles to go more than 10 minutes without checking their phone. Of the 2,000 people surveyed, one in 10 check their phones on average once every four minutes.

Four hours is the longest time the average person studied was prepared to go before the need to check their phone became too much. This alone is a true practice in presence and will be very difficult, but it will be very much worth the effort. Change your voicemail greetings, emails, and auto-text messages. Here is a sample message that works well:

Let everyone who needs to know that you will be "out of the office." It is important to have the support of friends, family, and coworkers. They need to know that you are not avoiding them, but that you want to enlist their support to keep all unnecessary and external pressures away. I recommend only checking your phone in the morning, afternoon, and evening. Avoid the inclination to constantly pick up your phone and check text, email, social media, or news. Those things will be there when you return. If anything, urgent happens, the world will find you. Turn off all technology 1 hour before you go to bed— no TV, phones, tablets, PCs, etc.

If you take a few days off, here is a perfect greeting to carve out time away from your old life: "I am away for 10 days and will have limited access to email and wi-fi. If you have an urgent issue, please call (someone you designate who has agreed to give you cover. This is very important) _____ or leave a message. I will return all calls when I return."

## *Your 10-Day Transformation Companion*

This book will be your personal manual. Dog-ear pages, highlight, and make notes in the margins. There is a section for journaling as well as a section to track your progress towards each area of intention every day. You will come back to this book again and again for references, to make notes from contemplations, and to capture your epiphanies. This book is your transformation companion.

# Notes & Epiphanies

# Chapter 7

## ~ THE 7 AREAS OF INTENTIONS ~

Now let's cover the 7 Areas of Intentions. A summary is below, and we go into more detail in the following pages. Each intention can stand alone and has its own benefits. However, all 7 used together create a powerful synergy.

This is the beginning of your awakening…

**Intention #1 – Meditation:**

Meditation is stillness and communion with the Universe. Meditate every morning and every evening.

**Intention #2 – Exercise:**

Movement is the lubricant for our bodies. Just 30 minutes every day is enough to regain energy & vibrancy.

**Intention #3 – Mindful Eating:**

Food is medicine and from Mother Earth. True wellbeing will be infused with each bite.

**Intention #4 – Self-Care:**

Prioritize and indulge. This is to remind you of your importance and significance. You are enough already.

**Intention #5 – Journaling & Daily Affirmations:**

Each day affirm your power and infuse it with the self-discovery of journaling.

**Intention #6 – Kindness & Gratitude:**

Do something extraordinarily kind. This uplifts the world. It is the law of Giving and Receiving.

**Intention #7 – Rest & Sleep:**

Get 8 hours or sleep or silence each day. This period of renewal results in more energetic living.

# Intention #1:

# Meditation & Mindfulness

During these 10 days, meditation is a key staple to your transformation. There are tons of meditation techniques, rituals, lengths, and so on. If you already meditate, continue your practice, ideally every morning upon waking and every evening, where you can find a place of solitude. Establish a routine practice so that everyone in the household respects that time and space. Put a note on the door if needed. "Quiet, please." "I'm meditating." "Do not disturb."

If you are new to meditation, take time in the planning phase to seek what resonates with you. The goal is to meditate twice per day—every morning and every evening.

I started in 2016 at the Cleveland Clinic Department of Integrative Medicine. They offered a class on the benefits of meditation and exposed us to various techniques. Since that time, I've widened and deepened my practice trying various styles. I started with 5 minutes and have sometimes meditated for over an hour. There is no right or wrong. The most important thing is that you have a daily practice to get centered and be still.

My hope is that you have or will develop a serious meditation practice, because meditation alone can and will lead you far beyond this 10-Day Transformation, higher and higher into the life you want.

When I talk about meditation, it's not just closing your eyes and taking deep breaths to relieve stress. It's much more than that. Meditation relieves you of your addiction to thinking so that you can connect with your spirit.

Your thoughts are not your own. They have been given to you by your environment, your family, teachers, friends, etc. You think differently than people across the world, or even across the street. Do you have the same religion, political party, or live in the same neighborhood as your family? This is not a coincidence. This is just how things happen. To break the addiction and find your purpose and truest self, you need to be present and slow down your mind's activity.

I like this definition from *The Buddhist Centre*:

> *"Meditation is a means of transforming the mind. Buddhist meditation practices are techniques that encourage and develop concentration, clarity, emotional positivity, and a calm seeing of the true nature of things. By engaging with a particular meditation practice, you learn the patterns and habits of your mind, and the practice offers a means to cultivate new, more positive ways of being. With regular work and patience, these nourishing, focused states of mind can deepen into profoundly peaceful and energized states of mind. Such experiences can have a transformative effect and can lead to a new understanding of life."*

Meditation is profound to transforming your life. It is restful awareness, not restful dullness. It is not sleep, and it is not zoning out while you're driving to work. It is focused attention on stillness. When you meditate alone, you create harmony and coherence for yourself. You also make a difference by radiating that harmony out into the world.

The world is a reflection of the collective consciousness of the people in it. The fact that you meditate and change your inner being, raise your consciousness, find peace, and practice love and harmony cannot help but also change the world. This is what is meant by saying that you are the light of the world. We each are—one by one and collectively—both at the same time. So, if you want to change the world, it starts by going within and changing yourself.

There are scores of information on mediation, but to get you started, here are some helpful tips. First, don't *try* to meditate. Just do it. Whatever you do is right for you at that time. Don't try *not* to think. You will think. All meditators think. The point is to slow the mind, because you can't stop it. I heard an interesting perspective that could help self-proclaimed overthinkers.

### *Meditation for Over-Thinkers...*

If you hate meditating because it is too boring and you can't stop thinking, try to focus on the *recovery* from thinking. Meaning that, when notice you are thinking about something, stop and give notice and recognition to what you are thinking about. That is the awareness that you are trying to achieve. In that moment of recognition, no matter how brief, you recover from thinking. That is the gap of meditation. Just practice awareness of your thoughts over and over. The meditation is in the recovering from each thought before the next one comes.

Here is what you are trying to do…

Compare your mindset on days when you are super busy to those days when you are on vacation. On one hand, you may have a to-do list that is 20 lines long. You're going from meeting to meeting, running errands, and taking care of family. On the other hand, compare that mindset to when you are on vacation and laying on a beach or leisurely strolling through a museum. Your thoughts are markedly slower, calmer, and more peaceful. Take that mindset to yet a further extreme into meditation, where you calm your thoughts even more—into quiet and stillness. Just like there are spaces in between each word you read on this page. There are longer pauses after each comma, and even longer pauses after each period. A longer pause yet even between paragraphs.

See. What. I'm. Doing. Here? Spaciousness. Meditation is the gap. It is a time of awareness where you live in those spaces. Eventually, the page of your life is less cluttered with words and punctuations and nouns and verbs. You become free. You feel your spirit, which is exuberant and boundless. You become a blank page and become reacquainted with your innocence. You become the infinite possibilities.

When you meditate, those spaces and gaps get longer and longer as you practice over the days, months, and years. In those spaces, your true self emerges, and there is more peace and harmony. There is also space at the end and beginning of each breath. Notice your thoughts work the same. There are spaces.

1. Select a comfortable space to meditate daily. Try to dedicate a place to use consistently. It will help you get into the flow quicker with time and will hold the energy of your prior stillness.

2. Sit comfortably in a well-grounded position, where you will not fall asleep.

3. Take 3-5 deep breaths to calm the mind.

4. Ask 4 essential questions:

   ➤ Who Am I?

   ➤ What do I want?

   ➤ What is my purpose?

   ➤ What am I grateful for?

Don't try to answer the questions. You are putting them into that tapestry of the Universe so that the answer can be brought to you sometimes during, but usually after, meditation.

The biggest frustration for beginners about meditation is they get easily distracted. Notice the distraction. Then observe your thoughts and let them go. You are not your thoughts. You can be with them and detached from them. This is why it is called a practice.

Over time, you will notice that you are no longer frustrated and look forward to the intimacy. Acceptance is the first practice of the day. You are able to set the tone with peaceful beginnings.

There are apps, books, and all types of programs and leaders that want to guide you through a meditation. After the clinic, I started at home with free-guided meditations online and via apps, and I've been on a journey of exploration ever since.

Start your journey, and find what resonates with you. Your exploration is the journey.

*"The degree of the absence of thoughts is the measure of your progress towards self-realization."*
*– Ramana Maharshi*

# Intention #2:

# EXERCISE

When did exercise become such a chore? When you're into it, it's really good, but once you fall off, it's like climbing a mountain. The key is to not take on this belief. All you want to do is move.

Just 50 years ago, there were no gyms, yoga studios, or treadmills. Exercise became more formalized once we started sitting around and watching those television sets. Today, with all these electronics and computers, exercise is the only way we seem to get any movement. But movement has always been essential. We're not rocks. We are made to move. Our heart and organs are constantly moving, even when our outside body has stopped. Get back into the rhythm of the world. Go on walks outside. Walk to the store or to the mailbox. Take the stairs or even just stretch. Sure, you can still go to the gym. I like the activity and the energy of other people around me.

I am guilty of sitting at a computer all day. I have to get up after an hour to walk around. Go stand outside and see the sun. Incorporate movement into your daily lifestyle. Feel your butt. Is it tired of carrying your weight? Stretch your arms out. Movement is about keeping your body well-tuned, which in turn keeps your mind crisp.

Don't think you have to go run a 5k or even a mile. Just start being mindful about your movements. You decide what is right for you. I got away from the scale, and I wear my Garmin for time and distance when I go on long runs or walks. However, I already know when I haven't been moving. My couch cushions sink in. My butt feels numb, and my stomach starts to sag onto my lap.

External measurements have their place, especially in the beginning. Once you become mindful, you can scan your body and know exactly where you are. You know if you've overeaten or been sedentary. External metrics can sometimes keep self-criticism high and self-love obscured. Be mindful. You already have all you need to know within you. The tightness of your clothes lets you know, as will the popping of those joints and the swelling of the ankles. The goal is to love yourself from the inside out, and then the approval you get from the scale, evaluations, and any other grading system becomes obsolete. You are your own answer. During these 10 days, you will move intentionally every day. Remember, even though this is an at-home transformation retreat, your activity level is a major part of your awakening. A clean and vibrant body provides the pristine opening to receive a perspective that may have been closed before. It is the fertilizer for that aha! moment to be born.

Exercise deliberately every day. The activity level you start with will determine what is right for you. If you already work out regularly, consider upping the intensity or frequency. Or better yet, change the routine all together. If you run and lift weights, then try yoga. If you only do yoga, try riding a bike. Whatever you wish, but the goal is to dedicate a minimum of 30 minutes every 24 hours to moving intentionally.

Awareness is the foundation to transformation. Review the list of popular activities below. To begin your awareness practice, underline the activities you already do. Circle the activities you will incorporate into your transformation plan, and in the empty space, write down a new activity you want to explore.

| Biking | Basketball | Baseball | Football |
| Tennis | Swimming | Walking | Running |
| Yoga | Pilates | Kickboxing | Resistance |
| Tai Chi | Stretching | Spinning | Barre |
| Dance | Skating | Soccer | _____ |

If you aren't very mobile, do chair yoga or maybe get help with stretching. Schedule those physical therapy appointments you've been putting off. If you can't walk, do upper body exercises. If you can't use your arms, then try a stationary bike.

My son is a quadriplegic, and he has found equipment to keep moving and keep his muscles from stiffness and atrophy. I say this to blast all the excuses that one might want to try. This is your transformation, and you can move even if you need help. Transformation is about using our God-given talents and reaping the rewards and blessings, whatever they may be.

You will become more aware of your body. Take a mindful minute to enjoy the feeling of soreness here and there in your muscles. Feel the accomplishment of a workout completed, and be proud of yourself that you are energizing your body. Then luxuriate in the recovery time with a massage or a nap. I like to take a super nap from time to time, where I put on a big old t-shirt or favorite PJs, close the blinds, and get under the covers. In my own bed, alone. Ahhh! Feel the changes in your body and realize that your choices actually do produce results.

*"No one succeeds without effort. Those who succeed owe their success to perseverance."*
*– Ramana Maharshi*

# Intention #3:

# MINDFUL EATING

Mindfulness and meditation are sometimes used interchangeably. I understand that, but still keep them separate. To me, mindfulness is when you bring stillness and awareness to what you are doing, and meditation *is* stillness. Its nuanced. I imagine that for the truly enlightened, they are the same thing. Eating is one of the obvious things that we all have in common. Every person must eat to live.

Mindful eating has been the doorway to my awakening. So much so, that my first business is UGottaEat, a platform for sharing meals and eating freshly-made food. My first book is 366 Daily Affirmations entitled, *A Year of [ME], Mindful Eating to Improve Overall Wellbeing.* By just practicing mindful eating, we can eliminate so many of the sicknesses and ailments that bind us—physically and mentally. I like this definition from *Psychology Today*:

*"Mindful eating involves paying full attention to the experience of eating and drinking, both inside and outside the body. We pay attention to the colors, smells, textures, flavors, temperatures, and even the sounds (crunch!) of our food. We pay attention to the experience of the body. Where in the body do we feel hunger? Where do we feel satisfaction? What does half-full feel like, or three-quarters full?"*

In the planning section, you decided the type of eating regimen you wanted to follow during your transformation. On this journey you eat anything you want, except W.A.S.P. Again that's White flour, Alcohol, Sugar, and Processed foods. That is the first step. The second step is to trust your inner guidance and start discerning your own healthy food choices. Take some time for self-reflection:

You know when you are gassy or bloated from things you eat. Don't eat that. You know what breaks out your skin or makes you lethargic. Don't eat that. You know that chemicals and pesticides are toxic and poisonous. Don't eat that. You get the point. This is your at-home transformation retreat so be realistic and remember, this is your commitment to you.

## How can clean eating help me transform?

Your wellbeing and, therefore, your transformation includes your body, mind, and spirit. If your body is sick, clogged, and diseased, it will be hard for your mind to focus on anything other than that. The closer you are to eating whole ingredients, the better value food is for cleansing your body. I believe you already know what is good and what is bad for you, but you may lack the inspiration or discipline to commit.

There is no shortage of books, diets, and data on how you should eat for a healthy, energetic lifestyle. Therefore, instead of recipes and cooking hacks, we focus on this awareness: A healthy body is more receptive to spiritual guidance.

Given that, I will only share a few important guideposts that you can incorporate into whatever methods that spirit leads you to for YOUR body. These tips are a combination of my own Wellness Coach Training, common sense, and a lifetime of experience. In addition to mindful eating and avoiding W.A.S.P. foods, there are a few other mindful tips to accelerate your transformation into a life of wellbeing.

### Eliminate fake oils.

Fake oils throw off your body's ability to clean your blood and your body's ability to eliminate the extra sugar and fat that make you sick. These are called trans fats, hydrogenated oils, or polyhydrogenated oils. They are manufactured in a facility to increase shelf-life of products, and they are mostly found in processed foods. Just read the ingredients.

Only use oils that come from animals or plants. This one tip alone will eliminate 80% of all that's bad for you, and it will lead you to a healthier body.

### Avoid toxins and pesticides in your food.

This means buying organic and non-genetically modified foods (non GMO) when you can. I know it's more expensive today, but you will help stave off chronic diseases activated by external poisons. Long term, you will save in healthcare costs, prescription drugs, and sick time away from work. Even if you only buy organic for these notorious "dirty dozen," you will make a huge difference in your long-term wellbeing:

- Apples

- Strawberries

- Spinach

- Nectarines

- Grapes

- Peaches

- Cherries

- Pears

- Tomatoes

- Celery

- Potatoes

- Sweet Bell Peppers

## Practice Portion Control.

The average portion size is considerably higher than what a healthy body needs. Eat half of the portions served at restaurants. Skip the appetizers and share the entrées. Even eat the appetizer as the entrée.

It is the excess food and calories that are clogging our bodies and blocking our clarity and energy. Use smaller plates and bowls at home. This will help you visually and physically create your optimal eating portions. It's so simple, I want to cry. It works.

Beyond that, mindful eating is the entire experience. Here are best practices to incorporate during the 10 days while eating:

### Address the food.

1. See the full plate of food.
2. Breathe in the aromas.
3. Bless the food.
4. Bless the hands that prepared the food.
5. Bless the earth for the bounty.
6. Marvel in the infrastructure that got the vegetables and meat from the farm to your plate.
7. Bless the animal for its life for your nourishment.
8. Thank God for the provision.

### Appreciate the environment.

1. Give the food your full attention. No TV, no phone, tablets, or computers and no reading materials.
2. Dedicate the first mouthfuls to silence to experience the food.
3. Engage in light conversation after initially tasting each item.
4. Silently bless your dinner companions.
5. Take in your surroundings.

### Appreciate the food.

1. Taste each bite.
2. See how vibrant the colors are.
3. Identify the spices, herbs, and flavors.
4. Take small bites, chew, and swallow before next bite.
5. Notice the textures.

6. Notice the temperature.

7. Use your hands to eat or feel the food when you can (your mom would hate this!)

8. When finished, give God thanks one more time for the provision and the nourishment.

You will notice that you feel quite satisfied after these meals. It may feel weird at first. Resist the urge to check your phone. Leave it in another room, or turn it off. However, you may have family members that like to eat with the news on and chat at dinner. Make the adjustments that are comfortable to you. It's okay if the TV has to be on and you're not watching it, because you go within. You are practicing mindfulness. It's you, with You.

Transformation is finding inner peace, even when the rest of the world is frenetic. This is your best practice time.

---

*"There are only two mistakes one can make along the road to truth; not going all the way, and not starting."*
*– Buddha*

---

# Intention #4:

# DAILY AFFIRMATIONS
# AND JOURNALING

## *Journaling*

I've tried journaling over the years and never stuck with it. But now, I write more daily, and so everything I write is a type of journal. When I travel, I find it especially beneficial to have a journal with me. Invariably there is an event or an epiphany that I experience that makes me want to write about it.

My kids gave me a journal that had only a few lines available for each day, and the same day was on the same page for 5 years. I love this book. I can't write much more than things like "I had a lot of meetings, and it was a great day." Or, "Feeling stuck on this new project, realtor never showed up, and things suck." "Today is mom's birthday! I called her, and she sounded really happy. The family took her out for dinner. Yayyy…"

After lapping 1 year, I noticed one week was a bad week for me this year and last year. I've noticed other times where everything was going great, and energy was high! I also noticed that when you only have a few lines, you write the main highlights of the day.

This journal made me realize that it doesn't take a gazillion paragraphs in a leather-bound bedside journal to be worthy of the experience. The introspection and the feel of pen to paper is therapeutic in the stillness and reflection. I almost always write about what I am feeling, and I hardly ever about things. When I do, it mostly ends with an emotion. "Got a job offer. Exciting!" "I unpacked all day today. I'm so exhausted."

We tend to focus on our thoughts and overthink, but our true guidance is our emotions. It is our spiritual guidance system. You know when you are stressed that something is not right. You are not getting the result you wanted. Likewise, you know when you are feeling content that you are right where you are supposed to be.

In meditation, you watch your thoughts come and go. With journaling, you document your thoughts. Your thoughts are so important to how you see life. You believe it, and you can achieve it.

*As a man thinketh in his heart, so is he."*
*– Proverbs 23:7*

So, the discipline in transformation is to take our mind through a journey. We still our mind to receive guidance; we record our thoughts to observe our thoughts objectively; and then, with practice, we can choose our thoughts with mindful awareness. Yes, you can choose. This is transformation. Choosing the thoughts which align with the fruits of the spirit. There can be no doubt, even for the most jaded among us, that the universal power wants each of us to bear the Fruit of the Spirit.

Journaling provides reflection time to contemplate where we got it right and where we got it wrong. There are bullies, mean girls, sociopaths, and simply people that we disagree with on what is fair and how to live an honest life. This will always be the case. It is not our job to change them. It is our job to understand them—understand that they too have been conditioned by their surroundings.

We can only change ourselves, and this is also the goal of transformation: to rise above into the light of the peace that surpasses all understanding.

During these 10 days, you will journal at least once per day and more as the feeling hits you. At a minimum, you need to put on your journal page your mood in whatever shorthand you wish—be it a smiley or frowny face, a thumbs up, or a rating on a scale of 1-5.

## *Daily Affirmations*

Daily affirmations lift you up, bring presence, and center your focused attention to your own wellbeing. They are practical reminders to pay precious attention to positive and affirming thoughts, actions, and beliefs. They are also a spiritual mantra that opens the mystical gateway, aligning your intentions with the power of the Universe. My first book, *A Year of ME, Mindful Eating to Improve Wellbeing*, I describe affirmations like this...

*"For 366 days, these affirmations are inspirations to lead you towards the wellbeing of the body, mind, and soul. With these daily passages, you make an affirmation to yourself each day to better focus on your health—**physically** with what you eat and do; **mentally** with how you view yourself and others; and **spiritually** in how you fall into the flow of the Universe."*

Essentially, you are retraining your current mental state, by depleting old bad habits and self-perceptions, and refueling with positivity and power. Below are my favorite meditations that will begin each of the 10 days. You can and should always create your own as well, for the areas of your life that are crying out for change. Starting with these and making them a part of your psyche will dramatically improve your life for the better.

- ❖ I give my authentic self the permission to thrive!

- ❖ I am creating the life I want.

- ❖ My true spiritual self and my worldly self are in alignment.

- ❖ When I let go of attachments, I gain everything!

- ❖ I have power and strength, and I am transforming my life!

- ❖ Today I am giving attention to my positive features and being thankful.

- ❖ My motive for eating well aligns with my highest and best self.

- ❖ I am creating the future in the present moment.

❖ Gratitude allows me to harness the positive energy to receive grace.

❖ I believe and declare I am everything God created me to be.

> *"But the fruit of the Spirit is love, joy, peace,*
> *patience, kindness, goodness, faithfulness,*
> *gentleness, self-control: Against such things there*
> *is no law."*
> *– Galatians 5:22-23 (AMP)*

# *Intention #5:*

# REST & SILENCE

During *The 10 Days* get a lot of rest. I mean, go overboard when you can and feel good about taking naps too. At a minimum, you need to dedicate 8 hours to sleeping at night. I know people that brag that they only need 4 hours of sleep. That's not true. You may only get 4 hours of sleep, and you may still function on 4 hours of sleep, but you *need* 8 hours to be your best self.

Sleep lets your body recover and rejuvenate for the next day. All of the areas here are fundamental life functions that, instead of embracing and cultivating, we twist them into pretzels to bend to our own will. There is your will, and then there is God's omnipotent will. Happiness is where these two align, but which do you think is more important to your wellbeing? Where do you spend most of your efforts? We try to do things in our own strength. We are taking time now to reenergize and transform with a mightier power.

Here are a few laws that we can all agree on: We must eat. We must sleep. We must breathe. We must move.

It's like the approach you take going to school or encouraging your children in their schoolwork. If you have to go to school, then do your best. Yes, you can take school for granted and graduate with C's and a bunch of tardiness and absences; or you can apply some intentionality to being your best, and thereby improve your ability to evaluate and navigate the vagaries in the world. And yes, maybe get the job and lifestyle you desire.

We take for granted the things that our body does for us. We can live a more vibrant and healthy life when we take better care of our core functions, such as eating, sleeping, breathing, and moving, rather than choosing to ignore them. We overeat and eat processed foods; we don't get the required sleep we need; we don't pay attention to our breathing; and we've become sedentary. Maybe you can relate to one of these, but you don't think it applies to sleep. It does.

Ideally, you want to sleep when it's dark outside and maximize your waking hours for when the sun is out. The biorhythms of the world are calibrated to this cycle. Most of us have learned, and experience that the sun gives energy, makes things grow and that the phases the moon impact the waves in the ocean.

You and I are just as impacted by how the cycle of the planet impacts our energy and growth. Depressed people want to sit in a dark room, and happy people want to get out and do something. Not convinced? Ok. Sit in the light. Then go sit in the dark and compare the experiences.

You will have a solid rejuvenation practice in this 10 days. You may even welcome more sleep after a day or 2 of exercising and a little pampering. Go to sleep. Get 6-8 hours. This includes an elimination of all technology for 1-2 hours prior to bedtime. This is 10 hours of no communication with the outside world via technology. This is precious time to have real personal interactions. Have a tea with your neighbor or spend quality time with your family. Make a comfortable space. Surround yourself with nice fragrances and light some candles.

If you can't start out sleeping 8 hours, still turn off all devices and practice silence. The choice is yours. You don't have to go to sleep, but you have to be present. Many people feel they need the TV or some noise to sleep. This is conditioning. You didn't need it as a baby nor probably through school.

Reflect on when in your life you became reliant on the TV to go to sleep. Was it a lonely time? Did it comfort you when you heard it on in the other room where your parents were, and it made you feel secure? Explore when and why it became a crutch, and then use this time to release it. Be free enough to sleep without the blue light, the noise of the news, or commercials buzzing through your head. Sleeping with the TV on is a drag to your overall health.

Remove the impediments to your transformation. You are practicing stillness and silence.

For some, this will be the biggest challenge. I can already hear it: "Hey! But I need that time to do housework after my kids go to bed," or, "There is work to do, and a big presentation coming up." I cannot address all of the possible excuses, but I tell you this: Your lack of sleep is part of any resistance present in your life.

Rest and restoration will give you the stamina, the clarity, and the wisdom to solve the problems that confront you while you are awake. Those problems or decisions you have to make at work that take hours to think through will be solved in a fraction of the time when you have mental clarity. Those interruptions that used to break your train of thought will begin to add fuel to your thought process and spark even better ideas. Those keys that you can never remember where you put them will always be where you think they are. You sharpen. You re-energize. You get back to YOU.

Remember, you are retreating from your normal activities with your eye on transforming your life into one of increased wellbeing, peace, and happiness. If you want to do the same things you have been doing, you will get the same result. That is not a catalyst for transformation.

Answer these questions for yourself:

> Is this a good time to go on a retreat (and if not now, then when)?

> Do I really want to transform?

Here are the guidelines, and they are super simple.

1. Schedule your 8 hours of sleep/silence.

2. Turn off all devices, including the TV, 1-2 hours prior to bedtime.

3. Go to bed. You can meditate, or you can journal. You can

spend quality time with your family…or you can sleep. You have free will and infinite choices. Choose wisely.

4. <u>Lights out.</u>

# *Intention #6:*

# KINDNESS & GRATITUDE

It is no accident that as I complete this section of the book that I am filled with an amazing sense of peace and gratitude.

*I feel the haze flowing around me like air, resplendent with thankfulness and knowing that all is well in this moment.*

*I release my need to know the outcome of all of my ventures, projects, and health issues.*

*I understand that out of infinite possibilities, I cannot possibly predict the amazing things that the Universe has in store for me when I get out of my own way. I am thankful and in the fullness of grace.*

*I am a channel for grace.*

*From my heart center I infuse these words and bless the reader at this very moment of consumption.*

*Grace permeates all things within and throughout this reading, infusing each letter with the power of the spirit within all of us.*

*You are touched at this moment.*

*Smile and let the blessing travel into your heart center and throughout your entire body.*

*Then send love and blessing back out to lift others.*

*The circle is complete.*

*You are a channel for grace.*

*All is well.*

*And so it is.*

*Amen.*

The conditioning of the world obscures our ability to recognize blessings and we forget to be grateful. When gratitude is genuinely animated from your heart center, you rise above your worldly diversions and are elevated to the realm where you see God's grace working in your life and you then experience joy. This is the realm where grace abides. *Gratitude lovingly and mystically lifts you up to receive grace.*

Grace is defined as an expression of divine love. It is the gift of your life that allows you to live the rich fullness of your potential. Amazing Grace. It is your life force and everything good within it, and gratitude is superhighway to receiving grace.

The Law of Attraction is at serious play here for your unfoldment into higher living. This law is that like attracts like, and what your give you also receive. Kindness towards someone is a physical expression of gratitude. Gratitude then lifts you into the realm of grace and illuminates all of the goodness in your life. In your joy, you continue to do more acts of kindness and extend feelings of gratitude, and the circle of life continues. You are lifted into your highest and best, most blessed self. It is beautiful and it is real.

## *Activating Grace*

Each of us is a channel for grace. But the blessing you receive comes *indirectly* from the connections with others, not from your own strength or sense of worthiness. This relationship is the thread that binds us and lets us live our best life. Kindness and gratitude is a superpower in your wellness repertoire, and it costs you nothing to gain everything. It is a simple and powerful practice.

In *The 10 Days* you practice *hyper*-kindness. This is not your everyday please, thank you and may I? This is going out of your way to be a blessing to others. The possibilities for goodness are endless. Every day send silent blessings out into the world—to loved ones, coworkers, strangers, politicians, even the person in the car next to you at the stoplight. Send handwritten notes. If someone compliments your bracelet, take it off, and let them have it. Give money to the beggar at the corner. Give cash and not coins. Be a blessing. Receive a blessing. Remember it is in your own self-interest.

You don't have to physically give anyone anything. To activate gratitude, you simply need to be grateful. You have to *feel* grateful. You have to *be* thankful. Hold on to that feeling and recall it as often as possible.

I could list the extensive medicinal benefits of gratitude. It improves sleep, reduces worry, makes us healthier, helps career advancement, increases friendships, increases self-esteem, reduces materialism, and on and on.

The simple and plain truth of the matter is that grace is everything—all encompassing. Everything rises when you are in grace. Why? Because you are living in your purpose and guided by the interconnectedness of grace—your true North.

## *Accessing Grace in Times of Trouble*

Okay, so you've lost a loved one, been laid off from your job, can't pay bills, have no love life, and you're scheduled for a biopsy next Tuesday.

Your question is, "How can I be grateful when I'm depressed?"

This may be the most important part of this entire book, because every single person in the Universe, from the beginning of time to the end of time, has and will have this experience. We share this experience in our oneness.

The key to getting unstuck is… a mustard seed.

Even the slightest expression of gratitude will change the entire trajectory of your life. Start with even a mustard seed size of gratitude. Be willing to see things differently. Your life just opened up to its infinite possibilities.

Do this exercise daily for far beyond *The 10 Days*. Choose 3 things for which you are grateful. Simply say 'Thank You' to the Universe. No matter how small. A flower. A skirt. Tickets to a game. The roof over your head. The juicy apple you just ate. If you like, you can even journal about them to increase the energetic power.

Imagine that each thing that you are grateful for is pleased and excited by your attention. Oh, it's so sweet. Feel the love. Animate the excitement and gratitude in your heart. Receive. You are now an active participant in the energy of giving and receiving from the quantum of the Universe.

Hold onto and revisit that feeling as often as possible. The law of attraction will begin to shower blessings upon you in relationship to your gratitude. Grace is supernatural, and it will *exponentially* overcome your situation. Give and receive. Your life is astounding. It is amazing.

# *Intention #7:*

# SELF-CARE

## *Is self-care selfish?*

*Not at all.* This is where we indulge, reward, and practice kindness and compassion to ourselves. It's the easiest part, but it's also where we struggle to feel good enough to enjoy it. Everyone comes before you—the job, the kids, the soup kitchen, etc. How could you actually take an hour to luxuriate and enjoy life? How could you not? Get this in your head—self-care is not selfish!

Athletes have to take recovery days. God rested on the Sabbath. Work used to be a 5-day week with weekends to recover, spend time with family, and take personal care. Unfortunately, our self-esteem and self-care has become secondary to an overworked and consumer-driven culture.

The work week has extended to 60+ hours a week, or to 6 days a week, or maybe you don't get any days off at all. Companies have shifted our culture to value profit margin over personal wellbeing. I understand that companies are in the business to maximize shareholder value, but that is a man-made construct that has been abused and can be changed. The focus on money over wellness is ironically making us sicker and poorer. We have less time and make unhealthy choices for the sake of convenience. Its code word is efficiency.

Social enterprises and non-profit organizations really embody the temperament of a holistic life, serving others, and therefore increasing individual self-worth and personal happiness. For-profit companies with a cause are now identified as social enterprises, and while they too want to make money, they are motivated by metrics that improve lives, like with meals served, homeless housed, trainings resulting in employment, vital services provided, etc. You can make money doing good. The concepts are not in opposition.

Focusing on work and consumerism has made money the #1 driver in our lives, not compassion, not family, nor God. This won't change overnight, but take a real hard look in the mirror to determine if you are caught in this loop.

Do you love it, or is it making you miserable? Ask yourself, what would you do if money were not an issue? What would you do if you could not fail? What would you do if you had no past? The answer is ANYTHING.

And through transformation you will more readily appreciate that you have infinite possibilities to live a happy life. Will you make the money you want? Will some people laugh at your ideas? Maybe yes, maybe no. But when you transform and live a higher life, those things won't matter. Then oddly enough, you will have everything you want.

> *"In order to gain anything,*
> *you must first lose everything."*
> *– Jane Hirschfield*

It is a difficult process to tear down the walls of conditioning that we have been raised with. Self-care and pampering is another very big step. You have to give yourself permission to go get that massage, take the bath, spend an entire afternoon reading or an evening star gazing... You have to believe that your recovery time is not a special indulgence, but it is a requirement. It will help you achieve all that you desire, and what you desire will change. You are not a bad or selfish person for practicing self-love. You deserve it, and this is your time.

Say YES! On every one of these 10 days, it is mandatory that you take time for self-indulgent behavior. While I don't consider a cleaning project all that indulgent, you might. Taking time to declutter that closet may be just what the doctor ordered. Freeing yourself from projects that are hanging over your head or the burden of their obligation can be a release. Indulgences make you feel good and are something you enjoy that is outside of your normal daily routine. You can go out and pay for someone else to do it, or you can do it yourself.

Here are simple things to enjoy:

- Massage

- Facial

- Manicure

- Pedicure

- Waxing

- New Hairstyle

- Star gazing

- Sensory Deprivation Tank

- Salt Bath/Caves

- Alone time at a bookstore or coffee shop

- Listening to music while stretched across the bed

- Netflix binge watching

- Lighthearted and Sci-Fi Movies

- Time in nature

## Practice Discernment

*Social Circles*

While supportive family and friends are important, during these 10 days, be very discerning about with whom you spend your time. The reason being is that it will be harder to break down your own walls, while being unconsciously pulled back into group-thought. If a night out with the girls is what you need, by all means, do it. Just stay clear of gossip, a victim mentality, and judgmental attitudes towards others. When you notice it steer the conversation to themes of positivity. If that doesn't work, then excuse yourself. You have that power.

This transformation is about finding, realizing, and using that power! Negativity is the film covering your vision from seeing what the Universe is communicating to you. It is the resistance to your own transformation.

Conversely, compassion is a strong healing elixir and helping friends and strangers in need can be a calming salve indeed. The love you give by being a comfort to someone who has lost a loved one or suffered a tragedy comes back to you in unknowable and immeasurable ways. Choose your circles wisely, not just during this period.

## Shopping

While it feels therapeutic and satisfying to get that new thing, it is also one of those indulgent habits, like overeating, gambling, smoking, or drugs that is used as a distraction or procrastination tool. During this transformation, it is important that we confront our problems, and do not run from them. This behavior drives the over-commercialism and, therefore, your long work weeks and workdays. Everything works together.

You will have time to contemplate these things for the deeper meaning during this retreat. Of course, if you want to shop as an indulgence for this retreat, then you should do it. Just remember that indulgence here is defined as something "outside" of your normal daily life. If you are a shopaholic, don't shop.

Transformation is about releasing the ties that bind you and keep you stuck in your life. You know deep in your soul if shopping is one of your binds. Choose wisely.

## Complaining

When you complain, you make yourself superior to someone, and you make someone else wrong. At the same time you make yourself the victim. It's the other side of the same coin. When aggrieved, the victim makes their grievances more important than others' and, therefore, superior in their predicament.

Trust me when I tell you that every person you have met, and will ever meet, has suffered and been mistreated in their lifetime. Everyone. No one is immune, because good times, like bad times, are fundamental in this world. This is not to discount those who have suffered unspeakable abuses and atrocities. Those definitely need to be addressed at much deeper levels. I'm speaking of regular life, which includes the breakups, lost jobs, money woes, divorces, biases, failed projects, weight gain, and any other common, albeit unfortunate, life events that don't go your way.

On the journey to your higher self, you will spend time coming to grips with this reality. You are above no one and beneath no one. We essentially all come from the same place [Understanding #1].

When you catch yourself complaining, stop and identify the superior-victim that is present. From here forward, you own your own choices. It is imperative to practice forgiveness and a non-judgmental spirit for the choices of others that don't align with yours. You are beginning to understand that everyone is just trying to do the best they can with the hand they have been dealt—just like you are. Spend time thinking about who needs to forgive you, and why.

## *Indulge*

This journey is about awareness and balance. We tend to take care of everyone else before ourselves, and we also tend to complain about it too. Let's leave that baggage outside of our transformation window, and work to not pick it back up on our way out.

*"Show me your Original Face, the face you had before your parents were born."*

*– A Zen Koan*

# Notes & Epiphanies

# Chapter 8

## ~THE RETREAT AGENDA ~

### Keeping Track

The activities for *The 10 Days* have essentially already been provided in the 7 Areas of Intentions. However, the details are yours to develop. Making these choices that arise out of awareness is an important part of your journey. You are in control of your destiny. You always have been, and here you finally assert your decision-making for your own wellbeing.

You have all the ingredients, and now just need to put them together—like baking a cake. While hard metrics can be discouraging rather than reaffirming, a daily points guideline is provided to assist you in achieving your optimal wellness. You have the ingredients; the points are the measurements.

The time for this transformation experience to come to fruition is 10 days. Strive to focus on each one of the 7 Areas of Intentions every day. Don't get discouraged if you miss points for a single activity, but do pay close attention to your overall points. The points are an indicator of your commitment and the degree of your transformation experience. Here is where you learn to incorporate the life-changing intentions that will transform your life.

## *Daily Agenda*

*Morning*

## *Meditation (4 pts)*

The most important aspect of a transformative spiritual experience begins with going within as early as possible—often called Sunrise Meditation. You could start by asking yourself the 4 essential questions.

*Who am I?*

*What do I want?*

*What is my purpose?*

What am I grateful for?

Don't try to answer right away. First, go into your meditation. The answer will come when your spirit is receptive full of awareness, often outside of meditation. When you add an evening meditation to your daily routine, you truly begin to levitate beyond your current condition and transform to the next level.

Give yourself 2 points for each meditation. Strive for 30 minutes, but even 5 minutes of intentional effort will make an incredible difference.

Trust that God will meet you where you are and help you from there.

*"Because you have so little faith. Truly I tell you, if you have faith as small as a mustard seed, you can say to this mountain, 'Move from here to there,' and it will move. Nothing will be impossible for you."*
*— Matthew 20:17 NIV*

## *Daily Affirmations & Journaling (2 pts)*

Reflect on the Daily Affirmations and create your own in your Transformation Journal. What do you want? Set your intentions and cast them into the day and the quantum field. [Chapter 5, Understanding #3] This is most potent immediately before or after Meditation. Then journal about your most salient experiences.

### **Daytime**

## *Mindful Eating (4 pts)*

Eat nourishing meals that give you energy and do not leave you sluggish and lethargic. Avoid W.A.S.P. [White Flour, Alcohol, Sugar and Processed Foods]. You want your senses heightened, not dull, so your body is receptive to optimal spiritual guidance. Each daily avoidance is worth 1 point.

### Exercise (2 pts)

Move. Walk. Go out into nature. Give your body the gift of attention to strengthen, lengthen, and stretch. Breathe exhilaration into your cells with some type of activity at least 30 minutes per day.

### Self-Care (2 pts)

Indulge yourself. Remember that taking care of yourself is not selfish. It is the way to reconnect and affirm your internal light. Take time in comfort, indulging, new and refreshing activities. Celebrate yourself.

### Kindness & Gratitude (2 pts)

Immerse yourself in gratitude. Think of at least one thing you are happy about and relish the way it makes you feel. Hold on to that feeling and recall it as often as possible. Extend a kindness to someone. In The Law of Attraction you receive what you give. So give your best.

Evening

### Sleep (8 pts)

Get enough Rest. Bedtime allows for 8 hours of sleep or silence. Eliminate technology 1-2 hours before bedtime. Turn off cell phones, tablets, computers & TV. Do evening meditation and journal. Lights out. Each hour of sleep/silence is 1 point for a maximum of 8 points.

The agenda for the 10 days is yours to develop. This is an important part of the process. What could be wrong with that?

---

*"All things are lessons God would have me learn."*

*– A Course in Miracles, Lesson 193*

---

## *What to Expect When Transforming*

Track your points daily and compare them to the mood you recorded the previous day. Do you notice any correlations? Journal about it in the Transformation Journal section. You will experience emotional and physical shifts. Notice them and work with them as guidance, and not against them. Everyone differs, but these are common experiences you may have during *The 10 Days*.

### **Day 1:**

You're excited, hopeful, and optimistic.

### **Day 2:**

You're getting into the entire idea of transformation. It's important to journal how you got here and about Day 1. What are you feeling? Who are you? Why are you doing this?

### **Day 3:**

You're feeling a little off center. Maybe a headache from caffeine withdrawals and a little cranky for missing sugar and processed food. Take it easy today. Practice the Law of Least Effort (from *The Seven*

*Laws of Spiritual Success by Deepak Chopra).*

## Day 4:

You're rebounding and feeling energetic. Difficult feelings and emotions begin to emerge. Transformation depends on you going through these barriers and not around them. You will contemplate these things as they come up throughout the remaining time of transformation. This is the transformation process. It is the alchemy, and only you can do it. This process is just a guide to help you create the type of space in your life and in your body that allows your spirit to shine through a little more brightly and lead the way for your life.

## Day 5:

You're halfway there and noticing a little lightness in the body. Maybe you want something "good" to eat. You're waking up and starting to notice coincidences, signs, and synchronicities.

## Day 6:

You're starting to see yourself again when you look into the mirror. You may be vacillating between feelings of giving up, to fatigue, to being hopeful. Stay strong! You can do it!

## Day 7:

You've done some great things and are feeling accomplished! You're one week in and noticing a difference. You're feeling like a treat or reward is in order—like a piece of cake or a bottle of wine. Your goal is to push past this temptation and continue to press toward the mark.

Work through the discipline of remembering that your transformation depends on you filling yourself as completely as possible with light and love, and for as long as possible—at least 10 days to begin the rest of your life. You are doing good, but here is where many people slip back into old patterns. Here is the hump day. You can choose differently. Persevere.

*And so it is... that both the devil and the angelic*
*spirits present us with objects of desire to awaken*
*our power of choice.*
*– Rumi*

### Day 8:

Spend time with yourself. See how beautiful you are. See the beauty in what you previously considered flaws. See where they have actually helped you learn and grow.

Spend time in appreciation of your own awesomeness. Go backward in time and give thanks for each of the events that brought you here. Review your daily journals. Achieving this knowing is what will keep you present in the Now, and then you don't even have to worry about the future.

Transformation accelerates in gratitude. That is why prayer is so important. Prayers of praise and worship are so much more powerful than prayers of "I want this," and "I want that." But when they are wrapped together in spirit, they explode and magnify, like a beautiful ballerina turning into a sunset.

## Intensity Options:

*Take the next 2 days by storm. You may decide to intensify your focus by adding a mid-day meditation or workout. You can spend hours in total silence or eat only organic and raw vegetables one day.*

*You're opening the communication channel with your spirit so wide that you are being spoon fed all that you need to know. It's hard to stay here. It can be overwhelming. Stay present.*

## Day 9:

You're excited and can't believe tomorrow is the last day. You're feeling something between melancholy and peace—not really wanting to get back to real life. The pressures of the real world and the to-do list may be nipping at you. Put them in a box and place them aside. Stay present. They will be there tomorrow.

*"And which of you by worrying can add even one hour to his life? ...So then, do not worry about tomorrow, for tomorrow will worry about itself. Today has enough trouble of its own."*
*– Matthew 6:34*

## Day 10:

You've done it! Maybe you're wondering, Where is my epiphany? I feel rested, but not different. Journal how you are different from Day 1 to now. What have you learned? What do you want to do next with your higher consciousness awareness?

Actively determine your next goals. List everyone you will work to forgive. Take it easy, and treat yourself kindly. Play.

The amazing mystical manifestations will reveal themselves in the days to come if they haven't already. Notice the decreased pain, higher energy and newly minted optimism. Prepare yourself to be aware and be amazed. Continually show gratitude to continue the flow of blessings coming your way from here now and evermore.

Make a change to remind you of this spiritual transformation. Get a new hairstyle. Buy a bright shirt or dress. Rearrange the furniture in your bedroom.

## Day 11:

Go in peace.

## Day 30-60:

Reflect and be in gratitude for all the amazing things manifesting in your life.

---

*"Yesterday, I was clever, so I wanted to change the world. Today I am wise, so I am changing myself."*

*– Rumi*

---

# The Point System

The point system is the actual Recipe to Remarkable Wellness. The chart below lists the actual ingredients and measurements. The retreat is the sacred space to create your new life. It's your private kitchen or laboratory for change. The 10 days is the gestation or cooking time. Every day you have an opportunity to achieve 24 points allocated to each of the 7 areas of intention. They indicate relative importance and ensure the mystical balance. Each day, strive for 20 points or above for a truly transformative experience.

Achieving over 15 points indicates you are on the right track, and below 15 points, you probably don't notice much change and will achieve results consistent with the reprioritization.

Be sure to record your points in each day's Transformation Journal and in the summary sheet for each day, so you can visually see your trends.

# Transformation Zones

### Transformative: 20-24 pts

Feeling energetic and awake. Epiphanies, ideas, and creativity are coming at you from everywhere!

### Awake: 15-19 pts

Heightened awareness and presence. Missed a meditation or workout and maybe ate 1 or 2 things that are clogging your pathway, but overall you are more present about your actions, emotions and surroundings throughout the day.

### Average: 8-15 pts

You made a few changes but are still basically in everyday mode—still searching for the space to transform, and not quite committed to the effort. No worries. This is a process. Strive for 24 points tomorrow.

### Asleep: 8pts or less

Your ego is leading your life experiences such that you are not able to break down the barriers to inner peace. You're not getting the rest, and you are likely feeling like a victim and focusing on barriers instead of unlimited potential.

Read Chapter 8 and beyond for inspiration and rituals to release what burdens you. As long as you keep moving forward you are still on the path. It is all perfectly orchestrated.

# Daily Agenda

| | | |
|---|---|---|
| **Sleep & Silence** | **8** | **33%** |
| *Meditation* | 4 | 17% |
| *Mindful Eating: No W.A.S.P.* | 4 | 17% |
| *Exercise & Activity* | 2 | 8% |
| *Journaling/Daily Affirmations* | 2 | 8% |
| *Self-Care & Levity* | 2 | 8% |
| *Express Kindness & Gratitude* | 2 | 8% |
| *Totals* | **24** | 100% |

*Chapter 9*

# ~ TRANSFORMING
# WHILE WORKING ~

I deally, your first retreat is a full immersion with some vacation time or mental health days away from work included. Your life situation may not give you the space for this. The good news is that learning to live a life of awareness and wellbeing can be done wherever you are. You only need to integrate awareness into your daily life. This is much easier than it sounds, but doable. And so, you are ready to transform and take the extraordinary step of total integration *while working*.

Be easy with yourself. Ten days is the target for true transformation, but you can still have epiphanies and awakenings in 7 days, or even 5. It's like meditation. Ideally, you would meditate for 30 minutes, twice a day. But even if you only do 5 minutes, once per day, it will still have exponentially better results in your life than not meditating at all. If you shoot for 10 days and achieve 8 solid days, you will still reap huge benefits and will continue to strive for the full 10 days until accomplished.

Doing this transformation while working requires a real dedication to planning ahead. That includes your shopping for groceries and getting babysitters or someone in charge for while you are meditating. Plan to spend your quality time when the electronics go off. Put your daily meditations, workouts, and bedtime on your calendar. This type of planning will serve as present moment reminders and help to keep you on track.

Add the following type of calendar to your daily journaling to be much more detailed with your daily activities. It's only you being accountable to you.

## <u>DAY 1</u>

Date:_____ Weight:_____ Mood:_____

| | |
|---|---|
| **5:00am** | **Sunrise Meditation** |
| **6:00am** | |
| **7:00am** | |
| **8:00am** | |
| **9:00am** | |
| **10:00am** | |
| **11:00am** | |
| **12:00pm** | |
| **1:00pm** | |
| **2:00pm** | |
| **3:00pm** | |
| **4:00pm** | |
| **5:00pm** | |
| **6:00pm** | |
| **7:00pm** | |
| **8:00pm** | |
| **9:00pm** | **Silence/Bedtime** |

# Notes & Epiphanies

# Chapter 10

## ~ THE TRANSFORMATION JOURNAL ~

### DAY 1 AGENDA

Track your points daily and compare them to the mood you recorded the previous day. Do you notice any correlations? Journal about it.

### Morning

*Meditation (4 pts)*             *Your Points_____*

The most important aspect of a transformative spiritual experience begins with going within as early as possible—often called Sunrise Meditation. You could start by asking yourself the 4 essential questions.

- ➢ Who am I?

- ➢ What do I want?

- ➢ What is my purpose?

- ➢ What am I grateful for?

Then go into your meditation. Don't try to find the answer. The answer will come to you when your spirit is receptive and full of awareness, often outside of meditation. Meditate twice per day.

### *Affirmation & Journaling (2 pts)*          *Your Points_____*

Reflect on the Daily Affirmations and create your own in your Transformation Journal. What do you want? Set your intentions and cast them into the day immediately before or after Meditation. Points: 1 for daily affirmation, and 1 for Journaling

## **Daytime**

### *Mindful Eating (4 pts)*                    *Your Points_____*

Eat nourishing meals that give you energy and do not leave you sluggish and lethargic. Avoid W.A.S.P [White Flour, Alcohol, Sugar and Processed Foods]. You want your senses heightened, not dull, so your body is receptive to optimal spiritual guidance. 1 point for each food (letter) avoided.

### *Exercise (2 pts)*                          *Your Points_____*

Move. Walk. Go out into nature. Give your body the gift of attention to strengthen, lengthen, and stretch. Breathe exhilaration into your cells with some type of activity at least 30 minutes per day. Points: 2 for exercising at least 30 minutes.

### *Self-Care (2 pts)*                         *Your Points_____*

Indulge yourself. Remember that taking care of yourself is not selfish.

It is the way to reconnect and affirm your internal light. Take time in comfort, indulging, new and refreshing activities. Celebrate yourself.

### *Kindness & Gratitude (2 pts)*        *Your Points_____*

Immerse yourself in gratitude. Think of at least one thing you are happy about and relish the way it makes you feel. Hold on to that feeling and recall it as often as possible. Extend a kindness to someone. In The Law of Attraction you receive what you give. So, give your best.

## **Evening**

### *Sleep (8 pts)*        *Your Points_____*

Get enough Rest. Bedtime allows for 8 hours of sleep or silence. Eliminate technology 1 hour before bedtime. Turn off cell phones, tablets, computers & TV. Do evening meditation and journal. Lights out. Points: 1pt per hour of rest and intentional silence for a max of 8 pts.

### *Total Your Daily Points:* _____

# DAY 1

*I give my authentic self the permission to thrive!*

Date:                              Today's Mood:

*My contemplations allow me to clear my head and open my heart.*

_____

_____

_____

_____

_____

_____

_____

_____

_____

_____

_____

_____

_____

_____

_____

_____

_____

_____

# DAY 2 AGENDA

## Morning

**Meditation (4 pts)**                    *Your Points*_____

Meditate each morning (*2 pts*) and each evening (*2 pts*).

**Affirmation & Journaling (2 pts)**      *Your Points*_____

Reflect on the Transformation Daily Affirmation. Journal about your daily experiences with resonance.

## Daytime

**Mindful Eating (4 pts)**                *Your Points*_____

Eat nourishing meals Avoid W.A.S.P. (White Flour, Alcohol, Sugar and Processed Foods) (1 pt per letter avoided)

**Exercise (2 pts)**                      *Your Points*_____

Breathe exhilaration into your cells with some type of activity at least 30 minutes per day.

**Self-Care (2 pts)**                     *Your Points*_____

Take time in comfort, indulging, new and refreshing activities. Celebrate yourself.

**Kindness & Gratitude (2 pts)**          *Your Points*_____

Immerse yourself in gratitude. Extend a kindness to someone. Give your best.

## Evening

**Sleep (8 pts)**                         *Your Points*_____

Get 8 hours of sleep or silence. Eliminate technology 1 hour before bedtime. (1 pt per hour)

*Total Your Daily Points:* _____

# <u>DAY 2</u>

*I Am Creating the Life I Want!*

Date:                              Today's Mood:

*My contemplations allow me to clear my head and open my heart.*

_____

_____

_____

_____

_____

_____

_____

_____

_____

_____

_____

_____

_____

_____

_____

_____

_____

_____

_____

# DAY 3 AGENDA

## Morning

*Meditation (4 pts)*                    *Your Points*_____

Meditate each morning (*2 pts*) and each evening (2 *pts*).

*Affirmation & Journaling (2 pts)*      *Your Points*_____

Reflect on the Transformation Daily Affirmation. Journal about your daily experiences with resonance.

## Daytime

*Mindful Eating (4 pts)*                *Your Points*_____

Eat nourishing meals Avoid W.A.S.P. (White Flour, Alcohol, Sugar and Processed Foods) (1 pt per letter avoided)

*Exercise (2 pts)*                      *Your Points*_____

Breathe exhilaration into your cells with some type of activity at least 30 minutes per day.

*Self-Care (2 pts)*                     *Your Points*_____

Take time in comfort, indulging, new and refreshing activities. Celebrate yourself.

*Kindness & Gratitude (2 pts)*          *Your Points*_____

Immerse yourself in gratitude. Extend a kindness to someone. Give your best.

## Evening

*Sleep (8 pts)*                         *Your Points*_____

Get 8 hours of sleep or silence. Eliminate technology 1 hour before bedtime. (1 pt per hour)

*Total Your Daily Points:* _____

# DAY 3

*I am trusting in god's timing for my success!*

Date:                              Today's Mood:

*My contemplations allow me to clear my head and open my heart.*

_____

_____

_____

_____

_____

_____

_____

_____

_____

_____

_____

_____

_____

_____

_____

_____

_____

# DAY 4 AGENDA

## Morning

***Meditation (4 pts)***         ***Your Points*____**

Meditate each morning (*2 pts*) and each evening (*2 pts*).

***Affirmation & Journaling (2 pts)***      ***Your Points*____**

Reflect on the Transformation Daily Affirmation. Journal about your daily experiences with resonance.

## Daytime

***Mindful Eating (4 pts)***        ***Your Points*____**

Eat nourishing meals Avoid W.A.S.P. (White Flour, Alcohol, Sugar and Processed Foods) (1 pt per letter avoided)

***Exercise (2 pts)***          ***Your Points*____**

Breathe exhilaration into your cells with some type of activity at least 30 minutes per day.

***Self-Care (2 pts)***         ***Your Points*____**

Take time in comfort, indulging, new and refreshing activities. Celebrate yourself.

***Kindness & Gratitude (2 pts)***      ***Your Points*____**

Immerse yourself in gratitude. Extend a kindness to someone. Give your best.

## Evening

***Sleep (8 pts)***          ***Your Points*____**

Get 8 hours of sleep or silence. Eliminate technology 1 hour before bedtime. (1 pt per hour)

***Total Your Daily Points: _____***

# **DAY 4**

<u>Today, I Appreciate Everything With
Presence and Intentional Awareness!</u>

Date:                              Today's Mood:

*My contemplations allow me to clear my head and open my heart.*

# DAY 5 AGENDA

## Morning

*Meditation (4 pts)*                    *Your Points*_____

Meditate each morning (*2 pts*) and each evening (*2 pts*).

*Affirmation & Journaling (2 pts)*          *Your Points*_____

Reflect on the Transformation Daily Affirmation. Journal about your daily experiences with resonance.

## Daytime

*Mindful Eating (4 pts)*                *Your Points*_____

Eat nourishing meals Avoid W.A.S.P. (White Flour, Alcohol, Sugar and Processed Foods) (1 pt per letter avoided)

*Exercise (2 pts)*                      *Your Points*_____

Breathe exhilaration into your cells with some type of activity at least 30 minutes per day.

*Self-Care (2 pts)*                     *Your Points*_____

Take time in comfort, indulging, new and refreshing activities. Celebrate yourself.

*Kindness & Gratitude (2 pts)*          *Your Points*_____

Immerse yourself in gratitude. Extend a kindness to someone. Give your best.

## Evening

*Sleep (8 pts)*                         *Your Points*_____

Get 8 hours of sleep or silence. Eliminate technology 1 hour before bedtime. (1 pt per hour)

*Total Your Daily Points:* _____

# DAY 5

Date:                          Today's Mood:

_My contemplations allow me to clear my head and open my heart._

_____

_____

_____

_____

_____

_____

_____

_____

_____

_____

_____

_____

_____

_____

_____

_____

_____

_____

# DAY 6 AGENDA

## Morning

**Meditation (4 pts)**                    *Your Points*_____

Meditate each morning (*2 pts*) and each evening (*2 pts*).

**Affirmation & Journaling (2 pts)**       *Your Points*_____

Reflect on the Transformation Daily Affirmation. Journal about your daily experiences with resonance.

## Daytime

**Mindful Eating (4 pts)**                 *Your Points*_____

Eat nourishing meals Avoid W.A.S.P. (White Flour, Alcohol, Sugar and Processed Foods) (1 pt per letter avoided)

**Exercise (2 pts)**                       *Your Points*_____

Breathe exhilaration into your cells with some type of activity at least 30 minutes per day.

**Self-Care (2 pts)**                      *Your Points*_____

Take time in comfort, indulging, new and refreshing activities. Celebrate yourself.

**Kindness & Gratitude (2 pts)**           *Your Points*_____

Immerse yourself in gratitude. Extend a kindness to someone. Give your best.

## Evening

**Sleep (8 pts)**                          *Your Points*_____

Get 8 hours of sleep or silence. Eliminate technology 1 hour before bedtime. (1 pt per hour)

***Total Your Daily Points:*** _____

# DAY 6

*I consume only what nourishes my body*

*and brings me vitality!*

Date:                              Today's Mood:

*My contemplations allow me to clear my head and open my heart.*

_____

_____

_____

_____

_____

_____

_____

_____

_____

_____

_____

_____

_____

_____

_____

_____

_____

# DAY 7 AGENDA

## Morning

**Meditation (4 pts)**                    **Your Points_____**

Meditate each morning (*2 pts*) and each evening (*2 pts*).

**Affirmation & Journaling (2 pts)**                    **Your Points_____**

Reflect on the Transformation Daily Affirmation. Journal about your daily experiences with resonance.

## Daytime

**Mindful Eating (4 pts)**                    **Your Points_____**

Eat nourishing meals Avoid W.A.S.P. (White Flour, Alcohol, Sugar and Processed Foods) (1 pt per letter avoided)

**Exercise (2 pts)**                    **Your Points_____**

Breathe exhilaration into your cells with some type of activity at least 30 minutes per day.

**Self-Care (2 pts)**                    **Your Points_____**

Take time in comfort, indulging, new and refreshing activities. Celebrate yourself.

**Kindness & Gratitude (2 pts)**                    **Your Points_____**

Immerse yourself in gratitude. Extend a kindness to someone. Give your best.

## Evening

**Sleep (8 pts)**                    **Your Points_____**

Get 8 hours of sleep or silence. Eliminate technology 1 hour before bedtime. (1 pt per hour)

***Total Your Daily Points:*** _____

# __DAY 7__

_I choose joy!_

Date:                          Today's Mood:

_My contemplations allow me to clear my head and open my heart._

_____

_____

_____

_____

_____

_____

_____

_____

_____

_____

_____

_____

_____

_____

_____

_____

_____

_____

# DAY 8 AGENDA

## Morning

**Meditation (4 pts)**                    *Your Points*_____

Meditate each morning (*2 pts*) and each evening (*2 pts*).

**Affirmation & Journaling (2 pts)**        *Your Points*_____

Reflect on the Transformation Daily Affirmation. Journal about your daily experiences with resonance.

## Daytime

**Mindful Eating (4 pts)**                *Your Points*_____

Eat nourishing meals Avoid W.A.S.P. (White Flour, Alcohol, Sugar and Processed Foods) (1 pt per letter avoided)

**Exercise (2 pts)**                    *Your Points*_____

Breathe exhilaration into your cells with some type of activity at least 30 minutes per day.

**Self-Care (2 pts)**                    *Your Points*_____

Take time in comfort, indulging, new and refreshing activities. Celebrate yourself.

**Kindness & Gratitude (2 pts)**        *Your Points*_____

Immerse yourself in gratitude. Extend a kindness to someone. Give your best.

## Evening

**Sleep (8 pts)**                        *Your Points*_____

Get 8 hours of sleep or silence. Eliminate technology 1 hour before bedtime. (1 pt per hour)

*Total Your Daily Points:* _____

# __DAY 8__

*I am healthy and vibrant!*

Date:                               Today's Mood:

*My contemplations allow me to clear my head and open my heart.*

_____

_____

_____

_____

_____

_____

_____

_____

_____

_____

_____

_____

_____

_____

_____

_____

_____

_____

# DAY 9 AGENDA

## Morning

***Meditation (4 pts)***     ***Your Points*___**

Meditate each morning (*2 pts*) and each evening (2 ***pts***).

***Affirmation & Journaling (2 pts)***  ***Your Points*___**

Reflect on the Transformation Daily Affirmation. Journal about your daily experiences with resonance.

## Daytime

***Mindful Eating (4 pts)***    ***Your Points*___**

Eat nourishing meals Avoid W.A.S.P. (White Flour, Alcohol, Sugar and Processed Foods) (1 pt per letter avoided)

***Exercise (2 pts)***     ***Your Points*___**

Breathe exhilaration into your cells with some type of activity at least 30 minutes per day.

***Self-Care (2 pts)***     ***Your Points*___**

Take time in comfort, indulging, new and refreshing activities. Celebrate yourself.

***Kindness & Gratitude (2 pts)***  ***Your Points*___**

Immerse yourself in gratitude. Extend a kindness to someone. Give your best.

## Evening

***Sleep (8 pts)***      ***Your Points*___**

Get 8 hours of sleep or silence. Eliminate technology 1 hour before bedtime. (1 pt per hour)

***Total Your Daily Points: _____***

# **DAY 9**

*I practice forgiveness and gratitude every day!*

Date:                                Today's Mood:

*My contemplations allow me to clear my head and open my heart.*

_____

_____

_____

_____

_____

_____

_____

_____

_____

_____

_____

_____

_____

_____

_____

_____

_____

# DAY 10 AGENDA

## Morning

*Meditation (4 pts)*          *Your Points*_____

Meditate each morning (*2 pts*) and each evening (*2 pts*).

*Affirmation & Journaling (2 pts)*          *Your Points*_____

Reflect on the Transformation Daily Affirmation. Journal about your daily experiences with resonance.

## Daytime

*Mindful Eating (4 pts)*          *Your Points*_____

Eat nourishing meals Avoid W.A.S.P. (White Flour, Alcohol, Sugar and Processed Foods) (1 pt per letter avoided)

*Exercise (2 pts)*          *Your Points*_____

Breathe exhilaration into your cells with some type of activity at least 30 minutes per day.

*Self-Care (2 pts)*          *Your Points*_____

Take time in comfort, indulging, new and refreshing activities. Celebrate yourself.

*Kindness & Gratitude (2 pts)*          *Your Points*_____

Immerse yourself in gratitude. Extend a kindness to someone. Give your best.

## Evening

*Sleep (8 pts)*          *Your Points*_____

Get 8 hours of sleep or silence. Eliminate technology 1 hour before bedtime. (1 pt per hour)

*Total Your Daily Points:* _____

# DAY 10

*Eating well + awareness = happiness!*

Date:                          Today's Mood:

*My contemplations allow me to clear my head and open my heart.*

_____

_____

_____

_____

_____

_____

_____

_____

_____

_____

_____

_____

_____

_____

_____

_____

_____

# Transformation Tracking Summary

| Areas of Intention | Max | Scoring |
| --- | --- | --- |
| Meditation | 4 | 2 pts per Meditation |
| Exercise | 2 | 2 pts for 30 minutes |
| Mindful Eating (W.A.S.P.) | 4 | 1 pt per W.A.S.P. avoided |
| Self-Care | 2 | 2 pts for Self-Care including play |
| Journaling & Affirmations | 2 | 1 pt for each Journal & Affirmation |
| Kindness & Gratitude | 2 | 1 pt for Kind Act, 1 pt for Gratitude |
| Rest & Silence | 8 | 1 pt per hour of Sleep/Silence |
| Maximum Daily Points | 24 | |

# The 10 Days Summary

| Intentions | 1 | 2 | 3 | 4 | 5 | 6 | 7 | 8 | 9 | 10 |
|---|---|---|---|---|---|---|---|---|---|---|
| Meditation | | | | | | | | | | |
| Exercise | | | | | | | | | | |
| Mindful Eating | | | | | | | | | | |
| Self Care | | | | | | | | | | |
| Journaling & Affirmations | | | | | | | | | | |
| Kindness & Gratitude | | | | | | | | | | |
| Rest | | | | | | | | | | |
| Total | | | | | | | | | | |

*Chapter 11*

# ~ THE CLEANSING PRACTICES ~

## *Going Deeper*

You have in your hands a simple structure for daily devotion that will guide your transformation. The real benefit is that you get to customize it to your individual lifestyle. You know what is stretching you out of your comfort zone and what is keeping you in it. You feel it in your gut, and your intuition is sending all types of warning signs to avoid some roads and increasing the speed limit on others.

Everyone evolves at their own pace, and no two people are alike. So, if these meditations, daily commitments, and times in silence are still leaving you feeling that there's still got to be MORE, let me assure you that there certainly is. Seek and you shall find. Remember, infinite potential!

If you want to go deeper and focus more intensely on your transformation, here are other topics and areas to explore to incorporate into your retreat.

### **Practice Silence**

Dedicate 1 day, or several hours each day, to complete silence.

Incorporate one or all of the following:

- No television

- No internet

- No social media

- No music

- No speaking

- No reading

## Fasting

Eliminate foods for the entire 10 days or remaining days of transformation, or fast for 12 hours per day. You can just pick 1 day or all days that begin with the letter T. It's your plan.

## Detox

Cleanse your body of biological and environmental toxins. Consider eating only raw vegetables, eliminating meat and dairy, and consuming healthy smoothies

## Nature

Spend minimum of 30 minutes in nature every day.

## Practice Creativity

Flow and experiment with all forms of art.

## Other areas of exploration:

- Aromatherapy

- Crystals

- Meditations

- Chakras

- Reiki

- Astrology

- Energy Work

- Identifying Archetypes

- Animal Guides

- Tarot/Oracle Cards

On a wellness journey, there are teachers, coaches, speakers, guides, gurus, pastors, etc. Since you are at home, you have yourself, but you are not alone. There are other mediums that you can listen to that will introduce you to new concepts and broaden your horizons.

From here, you find more in your own way of thinking and not just the way that was given to you upon birth. Look for all topics, subjects, speakers, and areas of interest that appeal to you, and go for it! This is the freedom you have been searching for. It's time to create your own syllabus and explore. Everything is open to you.

*"Why do you stay in prison,*

*when the door is so wide open?"*

*– Rumi*

# Banish Harmful Thoughts Ritual

In her book, *Awakening the Guru Within*, Joyce Fennel provides a few spiritual exercises to "banish harmful thoughts." Harmful thoughts are resistant to your transformation. That phrase, "the devil made me do it," is kind of true. Negative thoughts, jealousy, intimidation, hate, resentment—they all come out of fear. There are really only two emotions: love and fear.

When you abide in love, you put yourself in a realm to receive enlightenment [Understanding #2]. Fear, on the other hand, well… let's just say, you don't. I am an optimistic person, laced with a thin frosting of worry. So for many days, I found myself struggling to stay positive. It was hard work. When I let my guard down for even a minute, I found myself in a stupor. I would strive to get to a place where I had a steady barometer. "The place to stay is warm, Tonya," Lucky said.

This banishing exercise helped me immensely. I was able to drop the emotional baggage that I didn't even know was weighing me down. It was as if I had 3 pieces of luggage and had to run with it to catch a flight in 15 minutes. Out of nowhere, a friendly and trustworthy porter came up to me and said, "May I take your luggage, and check it all the way to your destination? If you like, I can even have it picked up, and it will be at your hotel room when you arrive."

I didn't even know I was carrying that much weight around. I did not know that my heart was in my throat. That I was choking on a race for time—a race you can never win, because time is a mental construct, not a spiritual one.

Take a minute to visualize when you were fighting against time, like waking up late for work or running behind schedule to pick up your kids. What does that feel like in your body? Your heart rate rises, and the anxiety and stress cause hormonal imbalances. You respond with more than just your emotions. It's physiological.

This exercise let me exhale immediately, and miraculously, it gave me an inner peace that comes with someone taking all of your luggage and sending you on a first-class excursion. I am taking my own creative license to add my nuances to this exercise and make it my own, but the concept is essentially the same.

1. Collect any and all harmful, judgmental, depressing, or negative thoughts and feelings you have, and in your own handwriting, write them each on individual pieces of paper. List your unforgiving thoughts. Name the people who have harmed you, one by one, and their offense on each sheet. Wherever you find worry or embarrassment, write them down also so that they can stand alone. All resentment and negative feelings should be listed to begin the cleansing process. No one will read these but you, so be brutally honest with yourself. This is your opportunity for cleansing and renewal. Feel free to use a bullet point or dissertation format. Whatever

continues to move you forward.

2. Find a nice container. It can be a box, jar, bowl, your favorite mug, or whatever suits you, but give it some thought so that it has meaning to you.

3. Set this intention over the container: "Into this box, I place old thoughts that no longer serve me. I release them to the higher power's divine energy with gratitude for all the lessons they taught me. I release them without judgment to be cleansed from my life. I now reclaim this energy for myself, look forward with hope, and embrace the fullness of who I am."

4. Now take each piece of paper, read it aloud, and say, "This thought no longer serves me. I release it to my higher power and thank it for all the lessons it taught me." Then place it in the container. Repeat this for each piece of paper as you place it in the box. When all of your troubles are in the box, repeat the intention in #3.

5. Now destroy the papers in whatever way gives you a sense of finality. You can tear each piece into tiny bits, you can bury the box, or even burn them. Repeat the intention: "I release these old thoughts that no longer serve me to the higher power's divine energy with gratitude for all the lessons they taught me. I release them without judgment to be cleansed from my life. I now reclaim this energy for myself, look forward with hope, and embrace the fullness of who I am.

6.  Find a quiet space to complete your meditation. Find a comfortable meditation position. Close your eyes and take 3 deep breaths. Breathe in the light and draw positive energy fully into each cell in your body. Imagine that there is pure light coming from the sky through the top of your head (crown chakra) and washing over and into your entire body.

7.  Imagine a golden-white ball of light in the middle of your forehead (third-eye chakra). The ball has a sticky surface and is moving through your body picking up pieces of debris and remnants that no longer serve you—for example, thoughts, emotions, and pains in your neck, arms, abs… everywhere. Visualize the movement of this sticky ball vacuuming up all debris and residue from the top of your head to the bottom of your feet.

8.  Release the ball through the soles of your feet and see them go deep into Mother Earth. Say out loud and with gratitude, "I release this energy and its charge into the Great Mother to hold, for it no longer serves me in this life. Amen."

9.  Now imagine a golden-white ball of healing energy from the heavens. Let it wash over you, starting from the top of your head and bathe each cell, muscle, tissue, organ… Let it wash over you, cleaning your body and spirit with the light of healing and a flood of love from the divine.

10. Sit with this new reality. Feel the lightness in your physical,

emotional, and spiritual body. Sit with the new energy. Embrace your new reality, and be immersed in gratitude, always.

11. Close your meditation with your own prayer of gratitude and slowly open your eyes.

You chose to carry the weight, and now you have chosen to let it go. Congratulations!

You may want to do a voice recording of some of these steps, or its entirety, so you can follow along easily until you memorize it. You always have this at your disposal to use when negativity is weighing you down in order to get back to your higher self. Things may get so heavy you have to do it a few times, or at regular intervals. That's okay. It's always at your disposal.

---

*"Mercy... is twice blest.*
*It blesseth him that gives, and him that takes."*
*– William Shakespeare, The Merchant of Venice*

---

Bring this new energy into your life constantly, and with this new awareness, you will begin to notice opportunities and people enter your life that will catapult you into your next phase of wellbeing. I took my box of negative thoughts outside, put them into a ceramic pot, and burned them. As I sat and watched them become engulfed and incinerated in the flames, the smell reminded me of times as a child when I visited my grandmother in the country and we burned the trash. I felt her sitting with me and smiling. It was magical. Since then, she's been with me quite often—a true comfort indeed.

After you banish your negative thoughts, you will begin yet a newer path of enlightenment and transformation, and you will understand that you are a part of something much, much bigger than yourself.

---

*"Suffering follows evil thought;*
*joy follows a pure thought."*
*– Buddha*

---

# Notes & Epiphanies

*Chapter 12*

# ~ THE POWER OF FORGIVENESS ~

My godmother is the sweetest woman in the world. As she gets older, she is starting to forget things. On one visit, she lost her phone on the airplane. She was terribly upset as you might expect, but not about losing her mobile connection to the rest of the world. She just didn't want to lose her contacts. I tried to reassure her that she didn't need to worry about that because everything nowadays is in the cloud. She just needed a new phone, and it could be downloaded.

She looked at me and said, "Well, where is this cloud, and how will it get from there into my new phone?" It was too cute.

I said, "Well, Ma, I'm not quite sure how it works because it is kind of technical, but I can assure you that it does work, like when we talk on the phone how you can hear me even though there is no string connecting our two phones."

She said, "Ahhh, I seeeee what you're saying."

The same assurance is given to us by the Universe. The path to enlightenment comes through the energy of forgiveness and gratitude.

I am a student of *A Course in Miracles,* and it is from this study that I finally received my best understanding of forgiveness. The point of forgiveness is not for the sake of absolving others of the wrongs that were done to you. The point of forgiveness is to be the vehicle that carries you to enlightenment. You cannot find your peace, purpose, or closeness with God without forgiveness. There's no way around it. So ask yourself, *Who am I not forgiving?*

When you learn to forgive, it has universal application to every situation in your life. You forgive your ex, your old boss, your torturer, and yourself for all things all at once. It's not a forgiveness of each wrong. It's a washing away of judging others for their offenses and turning your face towards the loving kindness where only God abides. Once you grasp forgiveness, it works more like "All is forgiven." True forgiveness is always the same.

*A Course in Miracles* is 3 volumes, and it is a study for the foundation of inner peace. It is not a religion, but a training system that teaches you to cut through the negative thinking of the world (or the mitote in *The Four Agreements*) and clearly experience the light of God. The main volume is the Workbook, which is 365 lessons that teach you how to practically observe all of the concepts that will strip your conditioned thinking and then create a sacred space for stillness to bring you closer to God.

Essentially, God intentionally uses our relationships *not* to punish us, but rather to give us lessons for insights that bring us closer to Him. So unless you want to be mad at God all the time, then the fundamental lesson is this: Forgive, and you will see things differently. Set your prisoner free and then you are also set free to go about your own business.

Everything is a lesson to elevate your energy to a level of practice, where there is no malice. Then you will see things with inner peace, love, and harmony. This is the goal.

So remember, all things are within God, whether you see them as right or wrong. So to be closer to God, forgive perceived offenses, and you will see things differently. You will see the God side; you will learn the lessons; and you will thrive. It works in ALL situations. Would you stay mad at God? Remember…

❖ God does not learn. He knows all.

❖ God sees no contradictions. He does not perceive. All things are within Him.

❖ God puts forth lessons to help YOU learn, correct your perceptions, and bring your experience in line with what He has for you.

Consciously allowing yourself to be blessed by the lesson is forgiveness and gratitude wrapped together, all in one. Isn't God good?!

---

*"Consider it pure joy, my brothers and sisters,*
*whenever you face trials of many kinds,*
*because you know that the testing of your faith*
*produces perseverance.*
*Let perseverance finish its work so that you may be*
*mature and complete, not lacking anything."*
*– James 1:2-4*

---

Practicing creativity and visualizing what you want is key to its creation. You first have to believe that the vastness of the Universe is so awesome that, for everything you think you know, there are a million things that you don't know.

## Who Told You?

*You do not participate in the world fully.*
*You don't appreciate nature.*
*You don't care about the land.*
*You complain about the weather.*
*You over-consume and waste excessively,*
*clogging Mother Earth's pores.*

*You don't even pay attention to the day's gifts that*
*shower you with texture, movement, and velvety*
*richness.*

*You didn't even hear that wind that just whispered*
*to you.*

*You don't appreciate that chair that rises up to*
*meet you and comfort you after a long day.*

*You don't appreciate the value*
*of the food you eat all day, every day.*

*You dare get mad and cast blame for your idleness*
*and the weight you carry?*

*And still yet you stomp around*
*and expect favor from the world.*

*Why? Why is that?*

*Who told you that is how the Universe works?*

*– Tonya Kinlow*

# Notes & Epiphanies

# Chapter 13

## ~ AWAKENING ~

### Dark Night of the Soul

There will come a time, if you have not already experienced it, when you will feel all alone—like God is not hearing you, He's not answering, and you are flailing. If you're lucky, it only lasts a short while, but it will last for as long as it takes. What does this mean?

It is called a "dark night of the soul." After periods of faithfulness and failures, it feels like God has abandoned you. Even Jesus asked while on the cross, "My God, My God, Why have you forsaken me?" (Matthew 27:45)

This is a natural part of the journey. If you thought this was going to be a straight trip to Heaven without any bumps, bruises, or turns, get ready to recalibrate.

Life is the ebb and flow of experiences. Life is the totality of experiences of sensations, images, feelings, and thoughts. As you grow in your awareness, you begin to see these events not as good or bad, but as necessary learnings and visiting stops along the way.

It took three days for the resurrection of Christ. It took 40 years of wandering in the dessert for the Jews for a trip that should have taken merely 11 days. Jesus spent 40 days in the desert to fast and overcome temptation. All great transformations have a period of stillness, where growth is actually happening—a time of metamorphosis like a caterpillar turning into a butterfly. These are trying experiences that are necessary for growth.

---

*"Follow your bliss and doors will open
where there were no doors before."*
*– Joseph Campbell, The Power of Myth*

---

There are times of deep quiet, where the loneliness and silence can feel like an abyss. There is often a physical reaction as well. Your body may even begin to expel toxins and old wounds and injuries begin to ache. I get headaches and skin breakouts and my sciatica kicks in. Take care not to let yourself fall into the trap of depression or self-judgment.

The good news is that these are typically the times right before you have an epiphany and are elevated to a higher level of understanding. Trust that you are squarely in the process, albeit the difficult part. This is life. This is how it works. Trust the Universe, and it will not let you down.

## Transformation

Awakening to yourself is a natural process, like tearing away at muscles to make them grow stronger, or pruning wilted leaves so the plant can grow more vigorously. It is like getting enough sleep or rest to recover so you can have more energy the next day. The deep state is a human condition. Just know, you will overcome. Perseverance is the key. I have learned to practice forgiveness and gratitude when stuck. I ask myself, *Who am I not forgiving, and what would God have me learn?*

I went to school in Northern Florida, and it is common to have rain showers at any time. Then, an hour later, the sun is back out, and everything is dry as if it had never rained. If you are in a 90-minute class, you may never know it rained at all!

Once, while driving through a torrential rainstorm on the highway, there was very low visibility. My back-seat driver told me as long as I could safely follow that yellow line, I should turn on the hazards and drive slowly but not stop. Often the rain cloud is just sitting in one place. It just sits until its depleted. It could take 3 minutes or 3 hours, who knows? He explained that if I pulled over and tried to wait for it to stop, I could be waiting for a long time, but if I kept driving, I would eventually drive out of the rain cloud. It was so true, and I have become much more of an expert in my travels.

In the same way, once on this journey, you cannot stop. Slow down if you must. Put on the hazard signals, let the trucks pass you by, but do not stop. It's a dark night of the soul, but the sun will shine again. I promise.

The Universe is vast beyond comprehension. Imagine you lived in a house alone that is 10,000 times the size of the space you currently live in, without roommates or tenants, just your own space. The mind can't even conceive of that type of vastness on a personal level. What does anyone need with a house that's 1 million square feet? You'd probably close off most of the house, because its more than you can reach, or clean.

Even this is a minuscule metaphor for trying to understand the nature of the Universe. The ultimate word we use for the awesomeness of that which can't be named is God.

God transcends all thought. The mind cannot conceive it. Words are insufficient. Myths are mystical fields of metaphors of things that cannot be expressed in words, attempting to access transcendent understanding. Trust me, if you try to analyze and apply logic to the universal quantum field, you will only scratch the surface of a grain of sand and get a headache to boot.

Understanding at this level comes through emotions and intuition. When awakened, these energies transcend the natural sensorium and provide a knowing into the realm of the divine.

---

*"It happened in a second,*
*but it actually took a lifetime."*
*– Tonya Kinlow*
*(my best explanation of my awakening)*

---

Accept that the way to understanding God is not through logic or working yourself to death every day from sunup to sundown. Accept that finding the inner peace of communing with the Divine is probably 180 degrees different from how you are currently living your life. Finally, accept that allowing yourself to open up to magical, mythical, and mystical thinking is the practical way to follow a path of peace, happiness, and enlightenment.

Myths are stories from ancient times with themes that have informed humankind over the centuries. They provide guideposts for us on how to live our lives, that keep us from making the same mistakes as our ancestors and previous cultures. They contain creation stories, conflicts, separations, resurrections, and the search for meaning and significance.

Mythical characters and mystics inspire use of a different way of communicating, including storytelling and artistry, to connote something where words are insufficient. It gives you a line to connect you with the reality of what you are. Mythology transcends.

How wonderful are those fairytales and Disney movies with their magical qualities? Even the animation makes you use a part of your brain that the words of logic and science cannot tap.

Tune into your mystical and spiritual side. Lean into your religion at this time if that is a comfort for you. Just stay mindful that religion is based on duality—the duality of right and wrong. God works beyond that in the singularity of spirit. A good analogy is that every religion works like computer software and hardware compatibility. The belief of Jesus Christ as the only Savior works only within the Christianity hardware, just like Excel & Word work naturally in Microsoft, and like the Pages software runs on Macs. They all work, but within their own codification.

We get stuck when we forget the One Spirit of a loving Universe, and we say, "Well, all Mac users are going to Hell," or vice versa. When in the reality of existence, Macs and PCs can put out the same quality products, but simply by different methodologies.

Everything that happens is considered evil for somebody. When it rains, the farmer is happy, and the golfer is sad. So say a mystical "Yes!" to everything. This is essentially the teaching of the Tao—that life is opposites, and so we should live in harmony with both. Sometimes it hurts; sometimes it feels good. The happy person participates in all cases with goodness and with integrity and without malice. The suffering of the world is to be experienced, just like the good. This is the essence of life.

The direct path is not to be afraid and avoid trouble, but to accept all that is, as the way it has to be, and that it is the manifestation of the world.

In the next section, "Nuggets of Divine Wisdom," I provide a variety of writings from different belief systems that, in their most essential form, actually are the same beliefs. This is a great time to lean on the most powerful assurances of your own religion, and not just know them intellectually, but to live and practice the principles that serve you and the Universe as God intends. Be open to other omens, mythical stories, and religions that have been introduced to you and may spark your divine truth in a way that may not have been touched in prior teachings. Invite other myths and metaphors of love that can open up your mind and heart to a way it may have been closed to before.

*"Every religion is true one way or another.*
*It is true when understood metaphorically.*
*But when it gets stuck to its own metaphors,*
*interpreting them as facts, then you are in*
*trouble."*
— *Joseph Campbell, The Power of Myth*

# Notes & Epiphanies

# Chapter 14

## ~ NUGGETS OF DIVINE WISDOM ~

### *Understanding the Quantum*

This excerpt is from *The Science of Getting Rich* by Wallace Wattles. It is a creative, yet erudite explanation of Understanding #1. I recorded myself reading it, and I listen to it from time to time, lest I forget how the Universe really operates:

> *"There is a thinking stuff from which all things are made, in which in its original state, permeates, penetrates, and fills the interspaces of the Universe. A thought, in this substance, produces the thing that is imagined by the thought.*
>
> *Man can form things in his thought, and by impressing his thought upon formless substance can cause the thing he thinks about to be created. In order to do this, man must pass from the competitive to the creative mind. Otherwise, he cannot be in harmony with the formless intelligence, which is always creative and never competitive in spirit.*
>
> *Man may come into full harmony with the formless substance by entertaining a lively and sincere gratitude for the blessings*

*it bestows upon him. Gratitude unifies the mind of man with the intelligence of substance so that man's thoughts are received by the formless.*

*Man can remain upon the creative plane, only by uniting himself with the formless intelligence through a deep and continuing feeling of gratitude.*

*Man must form a clear and definite mental image of the things he is to have, to do, or to become, and he must hold this mental image in his thoughts, while being deeply grateful to the supreme that all his desires are granted to him..."*

# From a Return to Love

*By*
*Marianne Williamson*

*"Our deepest fear is not that we are inadequate.*
*Our deepest fear is that we are powerful beyond*
*measure.*
*It is our light, not our darkness, that most frightens*
*us.*
*We ask ourselves,*
*'Who am I to be brilliant, gorgeous, talented,*
*fabulous?'*
*Actually, who are you not to be?*
*Your playing small does not serve the world.*
*There is nothing enlightened about shrinking*
*so that other people won't feel insecure around*
*you.*
*We are all meant to shine, as children do.*
*It's not just in some of us; it's in everyone.*
*And as we let our own light shine, we*
*unconsciously give other people permission to do*
*the same.*
*As we are liberated from our own fear,*
*our presence automatically liberates others."*

### *Creation Stories... What have we forgotten?*

Imagine you're just a spirit, before you were born into your body. You and I and an infinite number of other spirits are all in this one big room, which was bliss and a total state of peace.

Your soul says, "I wonder what's outside the door over there?"

Everyone says, "Don't leave the room, little spirit. It's way better in here. You don't want to go out there!"

But you say, "Yes, yes. It's pulling me. I gotta go."

You step outside, and you are mesmerized with these little children people. It's kind of interesting, so you hang out for a while.

All too quickly, you tire of the wasted energy and the harsh environment. You call out to the other spirits, "How do I get back in?"

Well, you're so far away now, you can barely hear them. But you hear the collective call, "Just keep following the path you're on. You have to circle all the way around to get back here. Hurry up!"

So you begin the journey with the distinct intent of getting back to your big room filled with bliss and peace. However, along the way you start having experiences that distract you.

You decide to hang out with this family. There's a mother and father that give you love and care, which is the closest feeling you ever had to the bliss of the big room, and so you stay with them as long as possible.

Then you meet these people called friends, and they treat you better than your family, so you leave home to go hang out with them, get an education, and try to become as happy as they are.

They seem to be trying to make money and teaching you that this is the way to bliss. You want to be happy, so you want to get some of that money stuff too.

It reminds you a little bit of home, but you can't quite grasp it. So you keep trying, typing, and getting happy and satisfied. Then, it wears off, and you try again.

You start having other experiences, traveling, and spending time with people who make you feel good, because this feeling touches on the bliss and peace that you remembered from some distant time. It's now somewhere in the back of your mind.

One lovely day, you stop by a cute, little cafe and get a coffee and a sweet to comfort you. Coming out, you meet someone who makes your heart beat fast, and you have an instant physical reaction.

You think you're home. You profess, "I love you!" and you lose yourself in the new life with your own children people.

Soon, you have totally forgotten about the room of bliss and peace. You have forgotten where you came from and that you wanted to get back to that ultimate bliss.

Time goes by and that shiny love starts to wear off. The happy feelings start to fade, and glimmers from your prior life never last for long with these children people. So the journey becomes arduous. You get to a point where nothing lasts. Nothing makes you happier than the day before. There's never enough money or affection to satisfy your desires.

You dream about another time, and you have a knowing that there is something bigger that you forgot. Your light has started to dim.

Time goes by, on and on and on… After countless moments, you find that you are just wandering.

You ask yourself the questions: *Is this really all there is? Surely there is something more to life than this—experience after experience, going nowhere… Where am I going? What am I doing?*

Now the other spirits have been watching you and calling out to you constantly. Whenever you were unsure of a decision, they'd say, "Go this way! Do this!" When you were lost or sad, they'd blow you kisses and try to send you messages, but you couldn't hear them. You stopped listening, but they always had your back. They never stopped trying to direct you back home to the room of bliss and peace.

Eventually, you begin to dream of this place where there is constant joy, and one day you wake up and ask yourself the essential questions:

*Who am I?*
*What do I want?*
*What is my purpose?*
*What am I grateful for?*

This is the first step of your awakening. Life becomes about remembering. And so you start your journey back to that blissful room. By asking the questions, you became aware. You open yourself up to omens and glimpses of the truth. You hear your spirit friends through the series of coincidences and synchro-destinies, and you begin to follow their directions communicated so uniquely. But you have to stay present to receive the guidance.

Eventually, you stay present. You meditate day and night to hear the guidance. You follow their divine messages and quickly find your way back to the room.

This is what happens to our souls. The good news is everybody makes it back eventually. It may take a few lifetimes. You, by being here and being receptive to your friend spirit, are on the fast track.

Keep asking the questions and listening to the answers. Access to the room of peace and bliss are always available to you. Now you can enjoy the rediscovery of your higher spiritual self and the journey back home…

And so, it is.

## *Another Creation Story… Where did we come from?*

This is a variation of a creation story I heard on a Shamanic retreat in Sedona…

The Great Spirit was everything and nothing at the same time and completely happy in its wholeness. After eternities, it decided to give birth to itself and make some mini-me's. Quadrillions of sparks were created and individualized, and out of flames and sparks came more flames and sparks.

The mini-me's decided to play hide and seek with the Great Spirit. So they created things and went around playing and experiencing themselves, hiding in and around other sparks. They focused so much on the hiding, that eventually they created a separation from the Great Spirit and forgot that they were even playing a game at all! They couldn't return back to the Great Spirit because they had amnesia.

After an eternity, one mini-me said, I think there's something bigger. I feel that there is more, but I can't put my finger on it. Other mini's began to have similar feelings, and they all went about ways to explore and get rid of the amnesia.

When the swirling of energy got to a tipping point, instantly, a few sparks woke them up, and they remembered! When they told the other mini's about the Great Spirit, they were called lunatics and heretics. But as more mini-me's started to remember, religions were formed to help reawaken the ones with amnesia to bring them back in harmony with the Great Spirit. From the Great Spirit's perspective, they never left. The Great Spirit is everywhere.

This story is just like Adam and Eve, who after eating the fruit of the forbidden tree, forgot their connection and were separated from God. The Old Testament depicts the separation as a punishment for their sin. In many other creation stories, the separation is not a judgment, but more of a forgetting or an amnesia of God's children. Does an omnipotent God who is the Alpha and Omega judge Himself?

Whatever you believe, the most important point made in the New Testament, and many religions, is that God never leaves us. We may forget, but He is pure love and we only need to remember that to be in His fullness. It's the remembering that is the journey of our lives.

These creation stories unlock our creativity to connect with the Great Spirit. Quantum physics suggests that we are all just living a dream that God is having right now. We are a holographic image like on Star Trek. We are creating a reality out of the energy of our own desires. By changing our thoughts and beliefs, we return closer to the Great Spirit and wake up to become part of the Dreamer.

# Auguries of Innocence

*by William Blake*

*To see a world in a grain of sand*
*And a heaven in a wildflower,*

*Hold infinity in the palm of your hand,*
*And eternity in an hour...*

*Every night and every morn,*
*Some to misery are born.*

*Every morn and every night,*
*Some are born to sweet delight.*

*Every morn and every night,*

*Some are born to endless night.*

*We are led to believe a lie*
*When we see not thro' the eye,*
*Which was born in a night to perish in a night,*
*When the soul slept in beams of light.*

*God appears, and God is light,*
*To those poor souls who dwell in night;*
*But does a human form display*
*To those who dwell in realms of day.*

## The Beginning of _A Course in Miracles_

_"This is a course in miracles. It is a required course. Only the time you take it is voluntary. Freewill does not mean that you can establish the curriculum. It means only that you can elect what you want to take at a given time. The course does not aim at teaching the meaning of love, for that is beyond what can be taught. It does aim, however, at removing the blocks to the awareness of love's presence, which is your natural inheritance. The opposite of love is fear, but what is all-encompassing can have no opposite._

_This course can therefore be summed up very simply in this way:_

_Nothing real can be threatened._

_Nothing unreal exists._

_Herein lies the peace of God."_

---

_"There is a way between voice and presence_
_Where information flows._
_In disciplined silence it opens._
_With wandering talk it closes."_
—Rumi

---

## The Chinese Horse Parable

There is an ancient Chinese parable, which is a lesson in perspective and equanimity. This story is told over and over again, and if it is your first time hearing it, it will certainly not be your last…

One day an old farmer's only horse runs away.

His neighbor comes over and says, "This is horrible! I'm so sorry about your horse. How will you make a living?"

The farmer shrugs and says, "Who knows what is good or bad?"

The horse comes back the next day, and he brings with him 12 more strong, wild horses.

The neighbor comes back over to celebrate, "Congratulations on your great fortune!"

And the farmer replies again: "Good or bad… Who knows?"

Later, the farmer's ony son is taming one of the wild horses, and he's thrown off and breaks his leg.

The neighbor comes back over, "What a tragedy! I'm so sorry about your son. What misfortune you have!"

The farmer repeats: "Who knows what's good or bad?"

Soon the army is waging a war and comes through the village and forces all able-bodied young men to enlist and leave home for battle. But the son is spared because of his broken leg.

The neighbor says, "How lucky you are that your son was spared going into battle!"

And the farmer says, "Good or bad... Who knows?"

The moral? Life simply is. Life is an ever-flowing continuum of experiences. There is no good or bad, only perspective or judgment about experiences.

---

*"Out beyond ideas of wrongdoing and rightdoing,*
*There is a field. I'll meet you there.*
*— Rumi*

---

## *The Tao Te Ching*

"Tao (in Chinese philosophy) is the absolute principle underlying the Universe, combining within itself the principles of yin and yang and signifying the way, or code of behavior, that is in harmony with the natural order. The interpretation of Tao in the *Tao Te Ching* developed into the philosophical religion of Taoism."

*The Tao Te Ching* is an ancient text written by Lao Tzu. It is considered the single most important text of Taoism. It is a book of wisdom that focuses on acquiring deeper goodness and virtue by gaining self-knowledge and rejecting worldly standards.

I find the *Tao Te Ching* even more titillating by the legends around its author. Who is Lao Tzu? Is he one man or three? From questions around... Did he really exist? Did he have a purported legendary meeting with the philosopher Confucius? What is the mystery surrounding when and where he Lao Tzu died?

There are many stories, but Taoist traditions present that he was an archivist for the library of the Zhou Dynasty court, and being forced to write down his learnings gave birth to the *Tao Te Ching*.

As wisdom is universal, the creative expression though ancient texts are woven into our everyday lives, and we don't even know it. They hide in plain sight.

This text was written around 500 BC, over 2500 years ago, and surely you are familiar with the phrase, "What goes around comes back around." This phrase is *in* the *Tao Te Ching*. Taoism became a state religion in 440 AD.

All the wisdom of the world exists within us. Through stillness we gain access to the path of its realization, or to bits and pieces of it directly. The Tao is woven with the yin/yang and seeing the true nature of life in its paradoxes.

This excerpt, like the horse story, shows us that there are two sides to every coin and that the acceptance of both is the way to peace:

*"All in the world recognize the beautiful as beautiful.*

*Herein lies ugliness.*

*All recognize the good as good.*

*Herein lies evil.*

*Therefore,*

*Being and non-being produce each other.*

*Difficulty and ease bring about each other.*

*Long and short delimit each other.*

*High and low rest on each other.*

*Sound and voice harmonize each other.*

*Front and back follow each other.*

*Therefore, the sage abides in the condition of wu-wei*

*(unattached action).*

*And carries out the wordless teaching.*

*Here the myriad things are made, yet not separated.*

*Therefore, the sage produces without possessing,*

*Acts without expectations*

*And accomplishes without abiding in her accomplishments.*

*It is precisely because she does not abide in them that*

*they never leave her."*

## Koans—Wait... What?

Koans are paradoxical riddles, stories, or dialogues in Zen Buddhism that are used to demonstrate the inadequacy of logical reasoning, in order to provoke enlightenment. Koans stimulate your non-conceptual mind and call your spirit into your conceptualizations.

The point of a koan is not to answer it, but to stay with it until an answer is intuitively grasped. Here are a few that always hang in my consciousness.

*****

*Joshu asked the teacher Nansen, "What is the true Way?"*

*Nansen answered, "Every way is the true Way."*

*Joshu asked, "Can I study it?"*

*Nansen answered, "The more you study, the further from the Way."*

*Joshu asked, "If I don't study it, how can I know it?"*

*Nansen answered, "The Way does not belong to things seen nor to things unseen. It does not belong to things known nor to things unknown. Do not seek it, study it, or name it. To find yourself on it, open yourself wide as the sky."*

*****

A senior monk and a junior monk were traveling together. At one point, they came to a river with a strong current. As the monks were preparing to cross the river, they saw a very young and beautiful woman also attempting to cross. The young woman asked if they could help her cross to the other side.

The two monks glanced at one another, because they had taken vows not to touch a woman. Then, without a word, the older monk picked up the woman, carried her across the river, placed her gently on the other side, and carried on his journey.

The younger monk couldn't believe what had just happened. After rejoining his companion, he was speechless, and an hour passed without a word between them. Two more hours passed, then three, finally the younger monk couldn't contain himself any longer, and blurted out "As monks, we are not permitted to touch a woman. How could you then carry that woman on your shoulders?"

The older monk looked at him and replied, "Brother, I set her down on the other side of the river. Why are you still carrying her?"

*****

## Do Not Worry

I was raised a Christian. I have a great direct and personal relationship with God, and yet I find that I do not go to church as much as I used to. However, I do love spirit-filled church services. I even just love sitting in the peace of the spirit of the sanctuary.

For a long time, I was caught up in the external extremities that the church asked of me, such as… How often did I go to church? Did I give enough money? Did I go to Bible study? Which ministries did I join? Do I have the right outfit?

Now I've learned how to live a spirit-filled life, not from rules and regulations, but in the fellowship of the greatest two commandments that all the others hang on: *"…love the Lord God with all my heart, my soul, and my mind, and to love my neighbor as myself."* (Matthew 22:37)

I begin each day with meditation. I spend much more time in devotion, reflection, and contemplation throughout the week, than I ever did carrying my weekly religious duties. Even better than doing is living that life. I am walking the talk—doing the do. I believe. I finally have that sense of joy that the Bible always promised.

Before, I was too overwhelmed by the judgment of the church to receive the light, love, and encouragement that has been promised to me.

Now, with each interaction, celebration, and disappointment, I understand my significance in the Universe and my oneness with God. Every day, I grow more and more exuberant and downright giddy. It is simply delicious.

It is my fervent prayer that within this book, I am passing something on to you that will open up that direct line of being with me and you, and with you and God.

In my view, there are many paths to living a holy life. Many religions today, for their own survival, violently disagree. If God comes to save me directly, would you get in my way?

I offer you other perspectives to help you in your journey, which have helped broaden my thinking and elevated my life. My goal is always to offer an introduction to tools, notions, and exercises that will spark your own understanding—that you will awaken and hear the spirits calling out to you with guidance to get back to the big room of bliss and peace, that you remember how to get back to the Great Spirit.

From the time of great tragedy in my life, which included divorce and a horrific car accident for my kids, I found and held on to this scripture. I come back to it always…

## _Don't Worry; Tomorrow will worry about itself..._

[25] _"Therefore I tell you, do not worry about your life,_
_what you will eat or drink;_
_or about your body, what you will wear._
_Is not life more than food, and the body more than_
_clothes?_
[26] _Look at the birds of the air;_
_they do not sow or reap or store away in barns,_
_and yet your heavenly Father feeds them._
_Are you not much more valuable than they?_

[27] _Can any one of you by worrying add a single hour to_
_your life?_ [28] _And why do you worry about clothes? See_
_how the flowers of the field grow. They do not labor or_
_spin._

[29] _Yet I tell you that not even Solomon in all his splendor_
_was dressed like one of these._

[30] _If that is how God clothes the grass of the field,_

_which is here today and tomorrow is thrown into the fire,_
_will he not much more clothe you—you of little faith?_

*31So do not worry, saying, 'What shall we eat?' or
'What shall we drink?' or 'What shall we wear?'*

*32For the pagans run after all these things, and your
heavenly Father knows that you need them.*

*33But seek first his kingdom and his righteousness,
and all these things will be given to you as well.*

*34Therefore do not worry about tomorrow,
for tomorrow will worry about itself.
Each day has enough trouble of its own."*
*– Matthew 6:25-34 (NIV)*

# Notes & Epiphanies

## *Chapter 15*

## ~ FINAL WORDS ~

### Today is the day!

*The Manual for Living* by Epictetus (55-135 CE) is a set of excerpts that form the basis for his teachings. Epictetus was a Greek Stoic Philosopher whose focus was how to practically apply oneself on a philosophical level answering two questions:

- ➤ How do I live a happy, fulfilling life?

- ➤ How can I be a good person?

I pray that through your own study of yourself, your time with the spirit, and in prayer and meditation, you will come to know these wisdoms from the inside out. The biggest accomplishment here is to live what you believe. My prayer for you is that you take your revelations and new-found awakenings, apply it to your life and find inner peace. Your biggest transformation isn't what happened in the past 10 days. It is in front of you!

From the book, *The Art of Living: The Classical Manual on Virtue, Happiness & Effectiveness*, I leave you with the perfect quote from Epictetus' manual to end this book…

*"Now is the time to get serious about living your ideals. Once you have determined the spiritual principles you wish to exemplify, abide by these rules as if they were laws, as if it were indeed sinful to compromise them.*

*Don't mind if others don't share your convictions. How long can you afford to put off who you really want to be? Your nobler self cannot wait any longer.*

*Put your principles into practice—now. Stop the excuses and the procrastination. This is your life! You aren't a child anymore. The sooner you set yourself to your spiritual program, the happier you will be. The longer you wait, the more you will be vulnerable to mediocrity and feel filled with shame and regret, because you know you are capable of better.*

*From this instant on, vow to stop disappointing yourself. Separate yourself from the mob. Decide to be extraordinary and do what you need to do—now."*

And so it is…Your awakening.

# Notes & Epiphanies

# ~ *References and Resources* ~

## Books:

- *A Year of [ME], Mindful Eating to Improve Overall Wellbeing* by Tonya Kinlow

- *A Course in Miracles*

- *Awakening the Guru Within* by Joyce Fennel

- *Secrets of the Vine* by Bruce Wilkinson

- *Tao Te Ching* by Lao Tzu

- *The Art of Living: The Classical Manual on Virtue, Happiness & Effectiveness* by Sharon Lebell

- *The Holy Bible*

- *The Manual for Living* by Epictetus

- *The Science of Getting Rich* by Wallace Wattles

## Websites & Other Quoted:

- The Buddhist Centre: Buddhism for Today, "What is Meditation?" https://thebuddhistcentre.com/text/what-meditation

From Psychology Today:

https://www.psychologytoday.com/us/blog/mindful-eating/200902/mindful-eating

- Evan Campbell

- Jane Hirschfield

- Martin Luther King

- Ramana Maharshi

- Rumi

- William Shakespeare

# ~ *Recommended Reading List* ~

- *A Year of (ME), Mindful Eating to Improve Wellbeing*, Tonya Kinlow

- *The Alchemist,* Paulo Coehlo

- *The Seven Spiritual Laws of Success*, Deepak Chopra

- *The Four Agreements*, Don Miguel Ruiz

- *The Art of Living*, Epictetus

- *Finding the Guru Within*, Joyce Fennel

- *Ask and It is Given*, Esther & Jerry Hicks

- *Secrets of the Vine*, Bruce Wilkinson

- *A Return to Love*, Marianne Williamson

- *The Power of Now*, Eckhart Tolle

- *The Divine Matrix*: *Bridging Time, Space, Miracles and Belief*

- *Beyond Magic: Creative Living Beyond Fear*, by Elizabeth Gilbert

- *The Secret*, Rhonda Byrne

- *Sacred Contracts*, Caroline Myss

- *A Course in Miracles*, Dr. Helen Schucman

- *Siddharta*, Hermann Hess

- *The Bhagavad Gita*

- *The Seat of the Soul*, Gary Zukav

- *The Book of Joy,* Douglas Carlton Abrams, Dalai Lama & Desmond Tutu

- *You Are a Badass,* Jen Sincero

- *Conversations with God*, Neal Walsch

- *Eat, Pray, Love,* Elizabeth Gilbert

- *The Shack*, William P Young

- *Tao Te Ching*, Lao Tsu

- *The Dhamapada*

- *The Bible*

- *Meditations*, Marcus Aurelius

- *Poetry by Rumi*, Ellison

- *The Power of the Myth*, Joseph Campbell

- *Ram Dass, Fierce Grace*

## *Movies & TV:*

*Avatar*

*I Origins*

*Oprah's Super Soul Sundays*

Ask the Universe for guidance, and one thing will lead you to another, and another, and another. Before you know it, books will be falling at your feet, and you will be following your custom roadmap back to oneness with the Great Spirit.

# ~ About the Author ~

Tonya Kinlow is an Author, Transformation Coach, Blogger, and Inspirational Speaker. Her first book, *A Year of (ME) Mindful Eating to Improve Wellbeing* was published in 2017. She writes a weekly blog, *Mindfulness Matters*, raising consciousness for holistically living a healthy life. An avid foodie and mindfulness enthusiast, Tonya left Corporate America in 2016 to launch the UGottaEat app, creating an avenue for independent chefs to generate revenue while providing much needed fresh and healthy meals into their communities and providing access to food sharing. UGottaEat is dedicated to improving the overall health and wellness of society.

Before founding UGottaEat, Tonya was a Finance Executive with a corporate career spanning over 26 years. A crippling car accident involving her children led to her awakening and spiritual journey. She takes great pride in being from Washington, DC and a graduate of Florida A & M University. Her greatest joys are her children, Evan and Taylor, and her husband, Chef Craig Stevens.

Tonya spends her time writing, inspiring wellness through purpose, and building a system to feed and make the world a better place. She does 1:1 Transformation Coaching, leads Wellness Journeys and Inspirational Speaking and Trainings for groups and individuals.

Made in the USA
San Bernardino, CA
12 June 2020